access to history

HISTORY *and the* HISTORIANS

John Warren

Hodder & Stoughton

A MEMBER OF THE HODDER HEADLINE GROUP

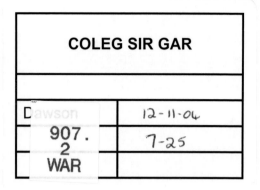
Orders: please contact Bookpoint Ltd, 39 Milton Park, Abingdon, Oxon
OX14 4TD. Telephone: (44) 01235 400414, Fax: (44) 01235 400454.
Lines are open from 9.00 - 6.00, Monday to Saturday, with a 24 hour
message answering service. You can also order through
our website: **www.hodderheadline.co.uk**

British Library Cataloguing in Publication Data

A catalogue for this title is available from the British Library

ISBN 0 340 67991 3

First published 1999

Impression number   10   9   8
Year   2004

Cover photo shows 'Pillars of Society' by Grosz reproduced courtesy of AKG, London

Typeset by Sempringham publishing services, Bedford.
Printed in Great Britain for Hodder & Stoughton Educational,
a division of Hodder Headline Plc, 338 Euston Road, London NW1 3BH
by CPI Bath

Contents

Acknowledgements

The Publishers would like to thank the following for permission to reproduce material in this book:

Abacus, for extracts from Primo Levi *The Drowned and the Saved*, 1989; Bobbs Merril, for extracts from Leopold von Ranke, preface to the first edition of *Histories of the Latin and Germanic Nations* in Iggers and von Moltke; Cambridge University Press, for extracts from Terrell Carver (ed.) *Marx: Later Political Writings*, G.R. Elton, *Return to Essentials*, 1991; Cape, for an extract from R. Barthes in S. Sontag (ed.), *A Barthes Reader*, 1982, Peter Gay, *Style in History*, 1975; Clarendon, for an extract from Peter Derow, in Simon Hornblower (ed.), *Greek Historiography*, 1994; Collins & Brown, for an extract from Roy Porter, in Juliet Gardiner (ed.), *The History Debate*, 1990; extracts from The Anglo-Saxon Chronicle, trans., GN Garmonsway, 1987, reprinted with permission from Everyman's Library, David Campbell Publishers Ltd; Fontana, for extracts from Lewis S. Feuer (ed.) *Karl Marx and Friedrich Engels: Basic Writings on Politics and Philosophy*, 1969, Lord Acton *Lectures in Modern History*, 1960; The Folio Society, for extracts from Edward Gibbon *The History of the Decline and the Fall of the Roman Empire* (ed.) Betty Radice, 1983; Granta, for an extract from R.J. Evans, *In Defence of History*, 1997; Harcourt Brace and Company Ltd for extracts from CA Robinson (ed.) *Selections from Greek and Roman Historians;* Harvard University Press for extracts from *Cicero, De Oratore* trans. Sutton and Rackham, 1952; HarperCollins Publishers, for extracts from H Butterfield *Christianity and History*, 1957; Pieter Geyl, *Debates with Historians*, 1962; Harvester, for an extract from M. Foucault, *Power/Knowledge. Selected Interviews and Other Writings, 1972-1977*, 1980; *History* LXVI, for an extract from R.H.C. Davies, 'The Content of History'; Lawrence & Wishart, for extracts from Christopher Hill *The English Revolution 1640*, 1940; Eric Hobsbawm, 'The Historians' Group of the Communist Party' in Maurice Cornforth (ed.), *Rebels and Their Causes. Essays in Honour of A.L. Morton*, 1978; Macmillan, for extracts Lewis Bernstien Namier *England in the Age of the American Revolution*, 1961, H. Kozicki (ed.), *Developments in Modern Historiography*, 1993; Manchester University Press, for an extract from N.J. Higham, *An English Empire. Bede and the early Anglo-Saxon kings*, 1995; Merlin, for an extract from E.P. Thompson, *The Poverty of Theory and Other Essays*, 1978; Methuen, for extracts from Denys Hay, *Annalists and Historians: Western Historiography from the VIIIth to the XVIIIth Centuries*, 1977; W.W. Norton & Company Inc, for an extract from J. Appleby, L. Hunt, M. Jacob, *Telling the Truth about History* copyright © 1994 by Joyce Appleby, Lynn Hunt and Margaret Jaco; Oxford University Press for extracts from Christopher Hill *The Intellectual Origins of the English Revolution*, 1965; Christopher Hill *A Turbulent, Seditious, and Factious People: John Bunyan and his Church*, 1989; Karl Marx *The Poverty of Philosophy*, 1980;

C.T. McIntyre (ed.) *God, History, and Historians: An Anthology of Modern Christian Views of History*, 1977; Penguin, for extracts from E. Said, *Orientalism*, 1995, Bede, *Ecclesiastical History of the English People*, trans. Leo Sherley-Price, Livy, *The Early History of Rome*, trans. Aubrey de Selincourt, Herodtus *The Histories* trans. Aubrey de Selincourt, Edward Gibbon *Memoirs of my Life*, (ed.) Betty Radice, E.P. Thompson, *The Making of the English Working Class*, 1968, Emmanuel Le Roy Ladurie, *Carnival: A People's Uprising at Romans 1579-1580*, 1980, Emmanuel Le Roy Ladurie *Montalliou. Cathars and Catholics in a French Village 1294-1324*, 1980, T.B. Macaulay *The History of England from the Accession of James II*, (ed.) Hugh Trevor Roper; Princeton University Press, for an extract from Walter Goffart, *The Narrators of Barbarian History*, 1988; Routledge, for an extract from K. Jenkins, *Re-thinking History*, 1991; Routledge & Kegan Paul, for extracts from Antonia Gransden, *Historical Writing in England, c.550-c.1307*, 1974; Royal Historical Society, for extract from G.R. Elton, *The Practice of History*, 1997; Thames & Hudson, for an extract from Orderic Vitalis, quoted in Beryl Smalley, *Historians in the Middle Ages*, 1974; University of Exeter Press, for extracts from Roger Ray, in C. Holdsworth and T.P. Wiseman (eds.), *The Inheritance of Historiography 350-950*, 1986; Vintage, for an extract from E.W. Said, *The World, the Text and the Critic*, 1983; Weidenfeld and Nicolson, for extracts from Ved Mehta *Fly and the Fly-Bottle: Encounters with British Intellectuals*, 1963; Yale University Press for extracts from R Kelley (ed.) *Versions of History from Antiquity to the Enlightenment*, 1991.

The Publishers would like to thank SITE/Architectural Association Photo Library for permission to reproduce the photograph on page 113.

Every effort has been made to trace and acknowledge ownership of copyright. The Publishers will be glad to make any suitable arrangements with copyright holders whom it has not been possible to contact.

Preface

To the Student Reader

History and the Historians is unlike any other book published in the *Access to History* series - it has been written with a very specific audience in mind. Its readers will be following a course or an element of a course which concentrates almost exclusively on historiography - the aspect of history which examines the way in which the subject has been researched and written about in the past.

The major implication of this concentration on historiography is that the book, as a whole, provides coverage of some demanding concepts and arguments. As a result much of this book will need to be studied in a different way from that advocated for other *Access to History* volumes.

Instead of reading each chapter rapidly in order to gain an overview understanding of the topic being considered and then working through the chapter a second time to consolidate your ideas on key issues, when using *History and the Historians* you will need to approach your first reading of each chapter rather differently. You may find it difficult to digest in a single reading all of the arguments presented in some paragraphs. Where this is the case, it is essential that you re-read the paragraph in question as many times as is necessary for you to understand what ideas are being presented to you.

In order to retain in your mind the relatively large number of points being made in each chapter, you will find in the end-of-chapter guidance sections explicit advice on how to overcome this problem by compiling notes in spider-diagram form as your reading proceeds. This advice is well-founded on experience.

You should find the extra effort required to extract the maximum benefit from this book to be well worthwhile. It has been planned and written with your particular examination needs specifically in mind.

Keith Randell

Introduction:
Asking Questions

It is perfectly possible to study history at sixth form or university level, or to have a genuine non-academic interest in history, without ever worrying about what history is. In fact, it is not only possible, but also rather convenient. One can choose to ignore those irritating questions which surface from time to time, like 'What is the point of studying history?' or, even more fundamentally, 'What is history?'.

This book was written with the assumption that it is foolish to ignore such questions - foolish, and fundamentally unhistorical. After all, those interested in history demonstrate their interest by asking questions of the past. Why did such-and-such an event happen? What was it like to live in this time or that? So, why refuse to ask questions about what it means to study history? In any case, we have no way of recreating the past to experience it ourselves - which is probably just as well. Since we cannot recreate it, we have to try to understand it through that special form of inquiry we call history. We therefore need to know what we are doing when we engage in that inquiry.

Of course, thinking about what it means to study history may well prove to be irritating, unsettling and time-consuming. Some historians have been reluctant to engage in such matters for this reason, and tend to be antagonistic towards those who want to consider history from a philosophical standpoint - a standpoint which might see it as a particular type of system of knowledge with methods which distill or distort the past in identifiable ways. And yet, nobody can write history without taking a stance, implicit or explicit, on what history actually is and what it is for. *History and the Historians* therefore not only offers a discussion of the writings of historians from the founding of the discipline of history to the present day, but also considers the vigorous modern debate on the nature and value of history.

Without in any way pre-empting these later discussions, I should, perhaps, propose a convenient working definition of history. We can start by drawing a straightforward distinction between the past and history. The past itself is logically irrecoverable: history can be defined as the study of the past and the attempt made (usually in writing, and largely by historians) to describe or explain it. Studying history, then, generally means studying the writings of historians - and often at second hand in a form regurgitated by teachers and lecturers: easier to take, perhaps, but sometimes a little thin and unappetising.

1 The Birth of Historiography and the Historians of the Classical Period

1 Assessing Historians

One of the most objectionable things we could do to the past is to assume that the people living in it were stupid. There is the temptation to do so, of course. People in the past knew so little, and the age of the micro-chip makes us arrogant and dismissive. Such arrogance we can, perhaps, guard against. But it might be argued that any attempt to assess historians is simply a more subtle form of judging them by present-day standards and finding them wanting. It would certainly be unwise to claim that we can totally disassociate ourselves from the attitudes and assumptions of our own society.

Assessing historians is therefore a rather tense affair. No assessment can take place without some criteria, and those criteria cannot be derived from some wondrous and timeless place where historians are always objective. In other words, any criteria we choose are bound to reflect our own time and the kinds of things our own society (or influential aspects of it) see as important. The criteria I have selected therefore reflect my own training in the style of history taught in British universities, my experience of teaching, my reading of various works which reflect the western liberal culture in which I live, what I think I know about the requirements of various examining boards and my acceptance of the political structures of British society.

Clearly, then, there are other possible criteria for assessing historians. I would argue that the criteria I have chosen at least allow us to do the best we can to assess historians on their own terms. They also allow us to evaluate historians in a reasonably structured and thematic way, and this makes comparison between historians much more meaningful. And, so, I have outlined below in question form the criteria I want to use.

i) What type of history is being written?
Is it, for example, largely a narrative of events based on the doings and sayings of political leaders? Or is it heavily analytical, concentrating, perhaps, on the economic structures of society rather than on telling a story of events? Does the historian put forward a particular theory explaining why change takes place?

ii) What historical techniques are employed?
What types of sources are used? Does the historian use a wide range? How does he collect them? Are they examined objectively? Does the

historian discuss the sources in any way? Are they mentioned in the text or as footnotes/references? Is the reader allowed to make up his own mind? Is the account balanced or biased?

iii) Language and style?
How readable is the historian? Are we offered clarity, or are the style and language more demanding of the reader? What readership does the historian target? Are the words and phrases chosen to arouse emotion in the reader? Is the historian trying to persuade? Is the tone neutral and calm, or perhaps sarcastic and angry? Is the historian striving for a literary effect?

iv) What does the historian see as the purpose of history?
Might the historian be seeking to use history as a practical guide with lessons for political or military leaders, or as a call to revolution? Does he see history as an end in itself - perhaps as a stimulus to imagination or intellect? Or does it try to meet the social or political needs of the ordinary citizens?

v) What impact has the historian had on historiography?
Did the historian stand alone, or inspire others to adopt a similar approach? Did he, in fact, found a school of history? If so, what developments within that school can be identified? Or did successors react against his approaches?

From what has already been said, I must obviously be prepared to admit that some of the above criteria are value-judgements. They might be used to label historians as 'good' or 'bad'. There is the tendency, for example, to assume that objectivity is central to the work of a good historian. This proposition is familiar enough to western liberals of modern times (whether they agree with it or not) but that does not mean it is true. An obsession with objectivity would certainly make little sense to a Roman writer of the classical period who was wanting to use history to teach certain moral and political lessons. His intention was to teach truth on his own terms, and we must recognise what those terms were. There is also the danger of looking down on historians who do not use what modern-day historians regard as appropriate scholarly apparatus. To do so would be ludicrous. It is possible to complain, say, about the Greek historian Herodotus because he failed to mention his sources in footnotes. This would be rather like criticising Julius Caesar's military strategy because he failed to use cluster-bombs and tanks. One must therefore make every effort not to use the criteria mechanically, superficially or with a sneering sense of the effortless superiority of the modern mind. This is why we must be careful to put the historian in the context of his own time: the time of which he was, of course, a product.

In summary, then, I have identified a set of criteria with which one can compare historians. These criteria are open to criticism - particularly on the grounds that they simply reflect my own present-day values. But they do at least make the necessary attempt - however flawed it might be - to evaluate historians on their own terms. Whether the attempt works or not can be judged by the following sections, in which the five-fold criteria are used to discuss, amongst others, those writers who might be seen as the founders of the discipline we call history. But it must be emphasised that the criteria are going to be used selectively and adapted appropriately. It would be absurd to try to force what I want to say into five paragraphs for each historian.

2 Herodotus of Halicarnassus (c. 484-c. 430BC)

a) The Political Context

The Greek town of Halicarnassus - the probable birthplace of Herodotus - lay just within the borders of the great Persian empire. Herodotus was keen to emphasise that he was Greek, but in using the word he was not referring to a unified country called Greece. What he meant by 'Greek' was a people with an identifiable and shared culture, language, religious system and customs. A Greek nation-state simply did not exist. The typical political unit in Greece was the self-governing city-state (*polis*). Despite their obvious cultural links, the city-states were usually keen to stress their differences. In political terms, some cities were ruled by kings, some by oligarchies ('rule of the few'), some by aristocracies ('rule of the best') and some took steps towards democracy ('rule by the people'). During the so-called Archaic period (from c. 700-500BC), the two most powerful cities, Athens and Sparta, demonstrated this diversity clearly. Sparta was ruled by kings, and most of its population were serfs, known as helots. The minority of male residents who were citizens of Sparta were educated and trained as warriors.

Athens had adopted political and legal reforms designed by Solon in the late sixth century BC. These centred on a constitution with some democratic elements - including the innovation of a People's Council, which at least gave the better-off farmers a voice in the city. However, this did not lead straight to full democracy: the General Peisistratos ruled as 'tyrant' (dictator) from 546-528BC. But his successors were overthrown in about 510 and, under Kleisthenes, the political role of ordinary freemen of the city increased substantially.

b) The Persian Wars (490-479BC) and The Peloponnesian War (431-404BC)

Athens grew in wealth and military power, with a particularly strong fleet. She dared to assist Greek cities in Asia Minor in a struggle to free themselves from Persian rule in the 490s. In 490, the Persian Emperor Darius I launched an attack on Athens which was defeated on the plain of Marathon. Subsequently, Darius' son Xerxes invaded mainland Greece in 480. Despite a brave defence by the Spartan Leonidas at Thermopylae, the Greek army retreated towards the Peloponnese. Athens was abandoned, but the Athenian fleet won the most crucial of battles near Salamis. With his fleet crippled, Xerxes retreated and crossed back into Asia. In 479, the Persians were defeated (largely by the Spartans) on land at Plataea. Xerxes' great empire had not been able to overcome the Greek city-states when they were forced into unity.

The Greek city-states had shown what could be done through co-operation, but the rivalry between Sparta and Athens was intensified by the obvious increase in the power of Athens. Sparta decided to launch a pre-emptive strike, and even formed an alliance with the Persians in the struggle (the Peloponnesion War). Athens was eventually defeated, but the Spartans decided not to destroy the city itself - as a token of her efforts in the Persian Wars.

3 Herodotus and his *Histories*

> Herodotus of Halicarnassus, his *Researches* are here set down to preserve the memory of the past by putting on record the astonishing achievements both of our own and of other peoples; and more particularly, to show how they came into conflict.

So starts the author of the work known to us as *Histories*, which was probably written some time during or possibly just after the Peloponnesian War. His introduction seems straightforward enough at first sight. We appear to have some sort of military or diplomatic history with an appropriate analysis of causes (given the reference to 'how they came into conflict'). Perhaps historians in our day might be less open about wanting to celebrate 'astonishing achievements', but it seems reassuringly familiar.

It is certainly true that Herodotus was concerned with military conflict. In particular, he looked at the uneasy relationships between the Greeks and non-Greeks (particularly the Persians) from the middle years of the sixth century. He started with Croesus of Lydia on the grounds that he was the 'first foreigner as far as we know to come into direct contact with the Greeks, both in the way of conquest and alliance'. Herodotus then discussed the rise of the Persian Empire under Cyrus (559–529BC) and concluded with the failure of that Empire (under Xerxes) successfully to invade Greece (480-479BC).

So far, so good. But now for some of the problems. The first and most fundamental is to establish what Herodotus meant when he used the word 'histories'. Its original usage by no means implied 'research into the past'. It could be used for any form of intellectual inquiry.

'Histor' (the adjective) carried the meaning of 'good judge' or 'expert' and certainly not 'historical' or 'historian' in the modern sense. Nevertheless, Herodotus used the word many times and it is thanks to him that its meaning as 'rational enquiry into the past' is established.

But how was this enquiry to take place? How was it to be transmitted? There were simply no set methods of researching or communicating an enquiry of this sort. Herodotus did not have access to written archives or the works of past generations of historians. Nor did he have a printing press to circulate his work in book form. Small wonder, then, that his main sources were oral, or that the *Histories* were intended to be read out aloud before an audience. This last point is made clear when we look at alternative translations of Herodotus' opening words. As the historian John Gould has pointed out, his first paragraph quoted above (from the very readable translation by Sélincourt) could be rendered 'What follows is a performance [literally, 'display'] of the enquiries of Herodotus from Halicarnassus.'[1] This certainly emphasises the oral element. And we might take a further example from the introduction to the *Histories*. Sélincourt's translation does not include the phrase 'without renown', and yet this is potentially significant. Herodotus wrote of recording those astonishing achievements so that they might not be 'without renown'. This phrase ties Herodotus in with the avowed aim of Greek epic poetry - to celebrate and commemorate the great deeds of men so that their reputations would never fade and die. The poems *The Iliad* and *The Odyssey* - whose supposed author was Homer - would have been familiar to every educated Greek. So, when Herodotus set out to write an enquiry into the past, he had no models to guide him beyond the fiction that was epic poetry and the related tradition of oral recitation. What influence did epic poetry and oral sources have on his work?

4 Herodotus and his Oral Sources

It is no surprise that Herodotus should, throughout his work, refer to extensive travels he had himself undertaken and to the way in which he collected data by interview. He named the places he had visited and - sometimes - referred specifically to individuals as the source of his information. Since the earlier parts of the *Histories* were dealing with the remoter past, he was of course collecting local oral tradition rather than eyewitness reports. For example:

1   About the oracles - that of Dodona in Greece and of Ammon in Libya
    - the Egyptians have the following legend:according to the priests of the
    Theban Zeus, two women connected with the service of the temple
    were carried off by the Phoenicians and sold,one in Libya and the other
5   in Greece,and it was these women who founded the oracles in the two

countries. I asked the priests at Thebes what grounds they had for being so sure about this, and they told me that careful search had been made for the women at the time, and that though it was unsuccessful, they had afterwards learned that the facts were just as they had reported them.

10 At Dodona, however, the priestesses who deliver the oracles have a different version of the story: two black doves, they say flew away from Thebes in Egypt, and one of them alighted at Dodona, the other in Libya. The former, perched on an oak, and speaking with a human voice, told them that there, on that very spot, there should be an oracle of Zeus.

15 Those who heard her understood the words to be a command from heaven, and at once obeyed. Similarly, the dove which flew to Libya told the Libyans to found the oracle of Ammon - which is also an oracle of Zeus. The people who gave me this information were the three priestesses at Dodona - Promeneia the eldest, Timarete the next, and

20 Nicandra the youngest - and their account is confirmed by the other Dodonaeans connected with the temple. Personally, however, I would suggest that if the Phoenicians really carried off the women from the temple and sold them respectively in Libya and Greece, the one who was brought to Greece ... must have been sold to the Thesprotians; and

25 later, while she was working as a slave in that part of the country, she built, under an oak that happened to be growing there, a shrine to Zeus; for she would naturally remember in her exile the god whom she had served in her native Thebes. Subsequently, when she had learned to speak Greek, she established an oracle there, and mentioned, in addi-

30 tion, that the same Phoenicians who had sold her, also sold her sister in Libya. The story which the people of Dodona tell about the doves came, I should say, from the fact that the women were foreigners, whose language sounded to them like the twittering of birds; later on the dove spoke with a human voice, because by that time the woman had stopped

35 twittering and learned to talk intelligibly. That, at least, is how I should explain the obvious impossibility of a dove using the language of men. As to the bird being black, they merely signify by this that the woman was an Egyptian.

On the face of it, this seems similar to the kind of techniques one might expect an historian to use today. Herodotus had acquired some information which his sense of reality led him to question. He then sought other viewpoints to challenge or corroborate (support) his information, and named his sources precisely. Next, he offered an hypothesis to account for the data. He also appears to have distinguished between myth or legend and facts about the past. Certainly, Herodotus seems to have subjected his sources to some meaningful critical scrutiny. However, we should temper our enthusiasm with a strong dose of caution. It has often been claimed that Herodotus was frequently unscrupulous in handling sources. Detlev Fehling[2], for example, has suggested that Herodotus appears to have tried to make his accounts seem more plausible or well-supported by simply inventing witnesses and their supposed comments. There are rather too many examples of convenient corroborative evidence - sometimes in cases where the content is so weird that no amount of corroboration can make it seem remotely likely. For instance, let us take a look at a splendid account of a Persian attack on Delphi. It seems that the unfortunate Persians ran into some rather unusual opposition:

1 … just as the Persians came to the shrine of Athene Pronaea, thunderbolts fell on them from the sky, and two pinnacles of rock, torn from Parnassus, came crashing and rumbling down amongst them, killing a large number, while at the same time there was a battle-cry from inside
5 the shrine. All these things happening together caused a panic amongst the Persian troops. They fled; and the Delphians, seeing them on the run, came down upon them and attacked them with great slaughter. All who escaped with their lives made straight for Boeotia. There is a story, I am told, amongst those who got away, that there was yet another miracu-
10 lous occurrence: they saw, so they said, two gigantic soldiers - taller than ever a man was - pursuing them and cutting them down. According to the Delphians, these were Phylacus and Autonous, local heroes who have enclosed plots of ground near the temple which are held sacred to them - that of Phylacus lies along the road above the temple of Pronaea,
15 and that of Autonous is near the spring of Castalia under the peak called Hyampia.

So, the account is supported by testimony from the opposing sides (Persians and Delphians), and the inclusion of the apparently impressive minor detail (geographical location) gives it the ring of truth. But then, we remember that we are being asked to swallow a very tall tale indeed. There is, at the very least, a strong possibility that Herodotus fabricated his witnesses to support a tale he had heard and enjoyed and wished to present to his audience as truth.

On the face of it, then, Herodotus employed a critical technique which is recognisable as part of the modern historian's armoury. And yet, when we look below the surface, it seems to be severely limited, inaccurate and, at times, little more than fiction. But such sweeping judgements are anachronistic (a very useful word meaning 'to take things out of their time and put them in an inappropriate one'). To assess Herodotus, we need to remind ourselves of the context in which he worked and not to condemn him because we work in an utterly different one. Firstly, we should recall our earlier point that his work aimed to preserve the renown of actual deeds in the past and so was unlikely to escape from the influence of the great fictional epics. We recall that the *Histories*, like Homer, was meant to be read out loud - and therefore had to exploit the techniques of oral delivery. As John Gould eloquently puts it, 'Herodotus' world is still the world of the teller of tales'.[3] Tales were told at times simply because they woke up the audience, were good to listen to and were particularly effective at demonstrating deeds of renown.

An essential part of the narrator's art is the speech. Herodotus used speeches because they added drama and pace and offered a vivid method of outlining a person's motives. Common sense, of course, tells us that they cannot be taken as literally true: neither Herodotus nor his sources were in a position to tape-record or take dictation *verbatim* ('word for word').

We now need to consider further the impact on the *Histories* of Herodotus' largely oral sources. They certainly explain his constant reference to 'having heard' or 'the facts I have heard reported' or 'there is a story, I am told'. More importantly, we need to appreciate that Herodotus was writing in many cases from the oral traditions of two main groups: great families and priests of the holy places. Gould has argued that he deliberately sought out people of similar social standing to those he was writing about: perhaps descendants of those originally involved. This in turn may explain inaccuracies where the family had preserved a tradition which exaggerated its own role in affairs. An example of this may well be an account of Zopyrus' role in the capture of Babylon. A descendant of that family was living in Athens in Herodotus' time, and it is possible - but not capable of proof - that Herodotus had made his acquaintance. This would also explain a number of references to that family (although it has to be admitted that Herodotus never actually said that he got his information from them). Also, problems of translation he experienced when using non-Greek sources may explain some of the wilder errors he fell into when discussing foreign cultures. And finally, the reliance on oral tradition may explain the need he felt to offer or to create that rather-too-convenient corroborative evidence. If there was no written evidence available - and there rarely was - then the listener had the right to expect proof in the form of oral testimony: and so Herodotus typically remarked 'I heard this from …'.

What this means, of course, is that we are getting a history of Greece and its neighbours which is to a considerable extent distilled through the perspective of fifth-century Greek élites. But Herodotus was not simply repeating stories told to him by various great families or custodians of shrines. Had he done so, his work would have been more like an anthology than a narrative. After all, as we saw in section 2, the local communities jealously guarded their sense of difference. In short, Herodotus transcended these differences and managed to create a reasonably unified narrative out of it all by using the Persian Wars as his central theme. It was a theme which made sense, because opposition to a common foe helped to bind the Greeks together.

5 Herodotus and Causes

Those who enjoy ticking off Herodotus (and they include his successor Thucydides) gleefully exploit the opportunity given them by his apparent use of legend and myth - particularly in terms of the events caused, it seems, by the direct and often wayward involvement of the gods in human affairs, such as the defeat of the Persians at Delphi. Students' essays are all too often labelling exercises where the black spot of 'supernatural causation' is slapped into Herodotus's unresisting palm. In my opinion, Herodotus did not state that the Gods did it all. He was, in fact, capable of a sophisticated analysis of human motives.

The issue of supernatural causation is a nevertheless a fundamental one. If Herodotus believed and argued that events were entirely shaped either by the whims of gods or by a kind of predetermined fate, then it certainly compromises the extent to which his work was a genuinely rational enquiry into human motivation and past events. It has to be said that his discussion was sometimes accompanied by what looks like an acceptance of the role of gods in human actions. For example, he discussed the reasons behind the decision of the Persian King, Xerxes, to attack the Greeks, and described the influence of his cousin Mardonius over the King, together with Xerxes' desire for glory and revenge. But Xerxes, it seems, changed his mind and decided that an attack would be a profoundly bad idea. No sooner was this decision made than Xerxes was visited by an exceptionally aggressive and unpleasant phantom whom he interpreted as a messenger from the gods. The phantom insisted in no uncertain terms that he should launch the attack. Xerxes then asked his counsellor Artabanus, who was against the invasion, to dress himself in the King's clothes and sleep in his bed to see if the phantom also appeared to him. And it did.

> 'Are you the man,' said the phantom, 'who in would-be concern for the King is trying to dissuade him from making war on Greece? You will not escape unpunished, either now or hereafter, for seeking to turn aside the course of destiny …'

The phantom stressed the point by preparing to burn out Artabanus' eyes. The unfortunate counsellor leapt up with a shriek and ran to tell Xerxes of the dream. Not surprisingly, the attack on the Greeks went ahead. It is tempting to use such examples as proof that Herodotus saw the gods as the movers of events and the humans as mere powerless victims. But this is not the case. The phantom, after all, was trying to force the humans to accept destiny (or fate). Force was needed because the humans had free-will. Fate might dictate what was to happen, but it was brought about, not by mindless automata switched on by the gods, but by complex humans who could and did ignore or misinterpret the promptings of the gods. Fate was still fulfilled, but by real human beings with their own thoughts and ambitions whose actions and motives therefore had to be explained. As Peter Derow puts it:

> ... predetermination - some version of fate, or thereabouts - may be a fact, but it is not an explanation, and Herodotus knew this. The explanation of human affairs has to be done at the human level.[4]

This seems fair enough, but it has to be said that there is a problem in generalising on Herodotus' treatment of the gods. There are one or two occasions where Herodotus unequivocally accepted their direct intervention. He spoke of the death of the sons of Spartan ambassadors (or heralds) in the Peloponnesian War as 'clear evidence of divine intervention' and an incident in which 'the hand of God was clearly to be seen.'

Perhaps we should conclude by suggesting that it would be wrong to argue that Herodotus' work was *severely* distorted by supernatural causation. Most of his explanations of why things happen were rooted in human behaviour and psychology, rather than the activities of gods. His work simply cannot be seen as a set of incidents connected only by the 'master-plan' - apparent or otherwise - of an all-powerful deity. Its fundamental structure is based very much on human relationships - in particular, a chain of 'obligation and revenge', to use Gould's phrase, stretching through and shaping the relations between Greeks and Persians. Things generally happened because political leaders reacted to a desire for vengeance, to honour family ties or to repay debts of various types. It is significant that the work started with a description of charges made by Greeks and Persians against each other over the alleged abduction of women. Herodotus was not prepared to accept the truth of these allegations, but, in mentioning them, he showed what he was looking for in history: in this instance, an origin of the conflicts in a desire for revenge.

6 Herodotus' Subject-Matter and Purpose

We have already noted that Herodotus was concerned to preserve the memory of past deeds of renown, and that this aim and the nature of his sources meant that the themes of obligation and revenge underpin his work. But Herodotus did not write a tightly-structured narrative based on those themes. An attractive curiosity - marked by his frequent exclamation that he was 'astonished' at various happenings - led him into lengthy digressions on the customs, religious practices and attitudes of non-Greeks. Some were better informed than others. And, of course, we have the story-teller's anecdotes. It is the earlier books of the *Histories* which contain myth or folklore: for example, abandoned Moses-like babies and the man (Polycrates) who threw his signet-ring into the sea to try to end an unnatural run of good luck, only to find it being returned to him in the belly of a huge fish. It could be argued that these various digressions did little for the progress of the narrative, and this is true. But there are gains.

Herodotus was doing more than dealing with political and military action. He offers to us a tremendously vivid insight into the mentalities of a Greek of his class through his descriptions of manners, customs, myth and geography. All the same, we should not overestimate Herodotus' range. After all, most of his work concentrates on explanation of events through an analysis of a network of personal relationships. This means that Herodotus was ill-equipped to tackle other types of cause, such as economic rivalry or class conflict.

Did Herodotus hope that people might learn in some way from his work? Did he have a lesson to teach about the causes of wars, perhaps, from which those involved in contemporary politics might gain a great deal? Were his comments aimed at a specific audience with specific concerns - perhaps the Athens of his time? The short answer is that, on the surface, he had no such aims. After all, there was no emphasis whatsoever in his own introduction on any intended message. However, it might be that, in his discussion of the causes of warfare, some generalisations emerged which military and political leaders might usefully have exploited. Since his work was produced against the back-cloth of the great conflict between Athens and Sparta, it seems at least possible that he would - consciously or unconsciously - have had things to say about war. However, I do not think Herodotus was in any way attempting to teach through his work. Even if we argue that preserving deeds of renown is, in fact, a way of glorifying war, it is clear that there are sufficient comments stressing the evil of war to counterbalance it. For example, when the Persian Cyrus captured the Lydian Greek King Croesus, he intended to burn him alive. He eventually relented, and then had a conversation (via a translator) which shows Herodotus at his most eloquent:

1 'Tell me, Croesus, who was it who persuaded you to march against my country and be my enemy rather than my friend?'
   'My lord,' Croesus replied, 'the luck was yours when I did it, and the loss was mine. The god of the Greeks encouraged me to fight you: the blame
5 is his. No one is fool enough to choose war instead of peace - in peace sons bury fathers, but in war fathers bury sons. It must have been heaven's will that this should happen.'

Our conclusion should be that Herodotus did not attempt to use the past to teach precise political or moral lessons. He expounded no laws of history through any attempt to provide a model of change or causation. His purpose, then, was to record the memory of great deeds of renown for his and future generations. But there is no evidence that he expected such deeds to be useful in any direct way. He had a story to tell, and he wanted to make it accurate because otherwise it would be pointless.

7 Was Herodotus the 'Father of History'?

Textbooks on historiography generally point out that Herodotus was given the title 'Father of History'. But what does it mean? The Roman writer Cicero (see pages 24-25) appears to have been the first to award it, and did so on the basis of making a distinction between history and poetry. History, he argued, aims at truth; poetry aims at pleasure. No doubt thinking of some of Herodotus' more dubious anecdotes, he was then obliged to point out that Herodotus was actually doing both. Some of Herodotus' successors felt that his willingness to include folk-lore and myth made him a doubtful parent of history. Cicero himself implied that Herodotus was a liar. He was also attacked in books with titles like *On Herodotus' Thefts, Against Herodotus* and *On Herodotus' Lies.* As we shall see, his near-contemporary Thucydides was keen to criti-cise the element of romance in his work. Hartog has commented on Herodotus' ambiguous position:

> In the last analysis, his position may be summed up in the following paradox: even though he is the father of history, he is not really an histo-rian.[5]

Fehling would no doubt agree. He draws an explicit parallel between Herodotus and Homer:

> Herodotus' idea was not to research the Persian Wars; he wanted to recount them as Homer had recounted the Trojan War. For him it was a matter of staving off oblivion rather than increasing knowledge.[6]

These judgements seem a little harsh. Perhaps Herodotus' great contribution is summed up in his statement of intent after the opening of his work and his description of the mythical abductions of Io, Europa, Medea and Helen of Sparta.

> So much for what Persians and Phoenicians say; and I have no intention of passing judgement on its truth or falsity. I prefer to rely on my own knowledge, and to point out who it was in actual fact that first injured the Greeks …

In other words, he was going to research the truth. The various objec-tions made to his technique and sometimes to his sincerity have not, in my view, proved that claim to be a fraudulent one. Thucydides' crit-icism of Herodotus was not, in fact, a denial of his influence over his successors but a recognition of it. Herodotus had established that the past should not simply be treated as a quarry for stimulating fiction, but that it should be respected in its own right: one should research what actually happened. Implicitly, this would mean near-contempo-rary history, since it was only for that period that the historian could investigate the sources himself. Herodotus had defined the nature of the enquiry and had attempted to realise it by (usually) distinguishing between myth and what we call history. He did so by investigating sources. In particular, he established that oral sources were the historian's best form of evidence, although his successors would limit that to eyewitnesses rather than including oral tradition. I would also argue that Herodotus established the view that history should not favour one side or the other, since this would obscure the truth. It has been alleged that his work favoured Athens, but there are sufficient occasions where Athens comes in for stern criticism for us to reject this view.

8 Thucydides (c. 460-400BC) and The Peloponnesian War

1   Thucydides, an Athenian, wrote the history of the war between the Peloponnesians [Spartans] and the Athenians, beginning at the moment that it broke out, and believing that it would be a great war, and more worthy of relation than any that had preceded it. This belief was not
5   without its grounds …

    On the whole, however, the conclusions I have drawn from the proofs quoted, may, I believe, safely be relied on. Assuredly they will not be disturbed either by the lays of a poet displaying the exaggeration of his craft, or by the compositions of the chroniclers that are attractive at
10   truth's expense …

    With reference to the speeches in this history, some were delivered before the war began, others while it was going on; some I heard myself, others I got from various quarters; it was in all cases difficult to carry them word for word in one's memory, so my habit has been to make
15   the speakers say what was in my opinion demanded of them by the various occasions, of course adhering as closely as possible to the general sense of what they really said. And with reference to the narrative of events, far from permitting myself to derive it from the first source that came to hand, I did not even trust my own impressions, but
20   it rests partly on what I saw myself, partly on what others saw for me, the accuracy of the reports being always tried by the most severe and detailed tests possible. My conclusions have cost me some labour from the want of coincidence between accounts of the same occurrences by different eye-witnesses, arising sometimes from imperfect memory,
25   sometimes from undue partiality for one side or the other. The absence of romance in my history will, I fear, detract somewhat from its interest; but if it be judged useful by those enquirers who desire an exact knowledge of the past as an aid to the interpretation of the future, which in the course of human things must resemble if it does not reflect it, I shall
30   be content. *In fine*, [in conclusion] I have written my work, not as an essay which is to win the applause of the moment, but as a possession for all time.

Later in his work, Thucydides reminded us of his authorship and provided some very useful background information.

1   The history of this period [ten years after the start of the war] has also
been written by the same Thucydides, an Athenian, in the chronological
order of events by summers and winters, to the time when the
Lacedaemonians [Spartans] and their allies put an end to the Athenian
5   empire ... The war had then lasted for twenty-seven years in all. Only a
mistaken judgement can object to including the interval of treaty in the
war ... So that the first ten years' war, the treacherous armistice that
followed it, and the subsequent war will, calculating by the seasons, be
found to make up the number of years which I have mentioned ... and
10   to afford an instance of faith in oracles being for once justified by the
event ... I lived through the whole of it, being of an age to comprehend
events, and giving my attention to them in order to know the exact truth
about them. It was also my fate to be an exile from my country for
twenty years after my command at Amphipolis; and being present with
15   both parties, and more especially with the Peloponnesians by reason of
my exile, I had leisure to observe affairs somewhat particularly.

So, we have an Athenian military officer - a general, no less - who wrote
mainly about a war with which he had been intimately involved.
Remarkably, he was able at least to appreciate the Spartan viewpoint, as
his exile was spent in Sparta. He was clearly, like Herodotus, making
full use of eyewitnesses. His comments on his sources and the hard
work he put in to discover the truth seem impressive. He claimed to
have tried to evaluate his own impressions - and those of others - by a
rigorous cross-checking, and also to have taken account of bias. His
reference to the lack of romance in his work might be seen as a deliberate criticism of Herodotus' inclusion of legend under the guise of
'what I was told', and his sarcasm about the truth of oracles would
suggest that the supernatural was to be treated with scepticism. But
what do we make of his comments about the speeches made by the
people in his history? He seems candid in admitting the difficulties in
remembering things *verbatim*. So, rather than claim that the speeches
were literally true, he decided to use them as a method of expressing
what would have been said given his knowledge of the background
circumstances. But then, we might ask, why bother with the speeches
at all? The point about the speeches aside, it is easy to see why
Thucydides has been claimed as the father of so-called scientific
history. He appears to have adopted an objective standpoint and a critical method to back it up. In practice, though, is the claim justified?

9   Thucydides and his Sources

The heart of Thucydides' history - and what he saw as the heart of
history itself - is the use of oral evidence from contemporary sources.
We have Thucydides' word for it that he found, assessed and
compared such sources. Unfortunately, he very rarely demonstrated
that technique in action. As we have seen, Herodotus was often

prepared to provide two contrasting testimonies and to explain the inferences he made. He was also prepared, on occasion, to leave it up to the listeners or readers to make up their own minds. Thucydides claimed to have done the work, but leaves very little trace. It is therefore tempting to argue that his claims to the careful collection and evaluation of oral sources are fraudulent. There is evidence to support this view - particularly Thucydides' readiness to tell us exactly what people were thinking and what their motives were. The historian Simon Hornblower discusses the issue, and concludes that it would be unwise to accept that Thucydides invariably researched his oral sources, although it would be equally unwise to argue that he never did. Of course, trying to identify where Thucydides did investigate his oral testimony and where he made it up is fraught with difficulty. Let us look at one specific instance: Thucydides' treatment of his opponent, the Spartan Brasidas, whose victory at Amphipolis had led to Thucydides' exile. Brasidas is treated with scrupulous fairness. His undeniable cunning was not used by Thucydides as an opportunity to savage him, and he spoke appreciatively of Brasidas' moderation and gentleness. He remarked:

> … the present valour and conduct of Brasidas … was what mainly created in the allies of Athens a feeling for the Lacedaemonians. He was the first who went out and showed himself so good a man at all points as to leave behind him the conviction that the rest were like him.

But the question then arises, from where did Thucydides get his apparent knowledge of Brasidas' intentions, strategies and motives? We simply do not know. One can point to his exile in Spartan territory, where he may have had the chance to talk to Brasidas. This can hardly explain how Thucydides knew so much about Brasidas' strategies and intentions in his later and final battle at Amphipolis, where he died. Hornblower asks the question:

> But can we really doubt that Thucydides talked to Brasidas, whom he handles sympathetically and with every appearance of possessing inside information?[7]

Given the confident detail, perhaps not. And yet, as we have seen, it is not necessarily the case that the whole of Thucydides' discussion of any one set of incidents was invariably the result of his scrupulous oral research. There must have been guesswork, and we cannot be certain how much. Maybe we can link this up with his treatment of the speeches: if necessary, making up some oral 'evidence' to fit what he genuinely thought must have been said or done.

10 Thucydides and the Purpose of History

It seems a reasonable assumption that, if a writer sees history as having a particular purpose, then that purpose is likely to be reflected in every aspect of his work. It might affect, for example, the choice of subject matter, the selection and use of sources or the imposition of a particular standard of 'truth'. Thucydides certainly intended to tell the truth about the Peloponnesian War because it was important to do so. He did not think that a bare accumulation of facts would be enough. Instead, his concentration on finding the truth behind what happened was important because he felt that it revealed certain things about human nature which it was vital for those who wielded any form of power to know. I very much take Momigliano's point[8] that Thucydides is not making some sort of simplistic statement that history provides a set of lessons in human behaviour. In fact, anyone reading Thucydides in the expectation of being provided with a convenient list of 'important things one has to know about human nature' is in for a great disappointment. But he was very interested, as one would expect of a military commander, in such matters as human responses in times of danger. His technique was to enter into the mind of his character and to discuss his feelings and behaviour. There is an excellent example of this in Thucydides' treatment of the Athenian commander Nicias before his great defeat at the hands of Syracuse in 413BC:

1   Meanwhile Nicias, appalled by the position of affairs ... and thinking, as men are apt to think in great crises, that when all has been done they have still something left to do, and when all has been said they have not yet said enough, again called on the captains one by one ... and adjured
5   them not to belie their own personal renown ...

On one level, this is fraudulent. Thucydides could not have known what was going on in Nicias' mind (especially as Nicias was butchered after his surrender and was therefore in no position to grant interviews). But, as a general himself, he presumably was able to estimate quite accurately his fellow commander's likely psychological state and to empathise with the situation. In short, Nicias was thinking what honourable leaders think and doing what honourable leaders do. If telling the 'truth' in this way led him beyond the mere narrative of events, then this is a price Thucydides was more than willing to pay: hence his willingness to write speeches which he could not have heard and, at times, to construct them in a dramatic and tragic style. It also explains the way in which Thucydides imposed a pattern on events, because events often follow from recurrent human behaviour. This suggests, of course, that there was some distortion of characterisation to meet the need for a pattern from which we can learn.

11   Thucydides' Contribution to Historiography

Without a doubt, it was Thucydides rather than Herodotus who had the greatest influence on their successors. In place of Herodotus' frequent and enthusiastic 'astonishment', Thucydides applied the coolest of cool reason. Herodotus enjoyed his asides and his stories: Thucydides offered a tight and disciplined narrative. Herodotus was willing to believe in the role played by gods: Thucydides was not. Herodotus was prepared to admit uncertainty and, at times, to let the audience make up its own mind: Thucydides was definite and told it what to think. Herodotus had an interest in the remoter past and tried to exploit oral tradition to find out about it: Thucydides gave us contemporary history and the eyewitness account. Where Herodotus invites us to an armchair for a fireside chat about great deeds, Thucydides has us sitting ramrod-straight on the edge of the chair whilst he tells us things we need to know. And in place of the Herodotean breadth of interest and readiness to write about legend, customs, geography, topography, non-Greek cultural history and, of course, the Persian Wars, we have one thing - political/military history. The Thucydidean concept of history triumphed over Herodotus, and, in the eyes of almost all classical historians, it was Thucydides, and not Herodotus, who wrote true history. In the longer term, we might expect both Herodotus and Thucydides to be revered and copied by the writers of the Renaissance, to whom the rediscovered classical civilisation seemed to offer an intoxicating truth and vision of the future through recovering the near-forgotten wisdom of the past (see pages 42-44). This was true only to a very limited extent. The later historian Polybius and other (arguably lesser) historians were preferred because their messages appeared plainer, their purposes clearer and their uses more immediate. The father of history and the father of so-called 'scientific' history had left some heirs of which they might not have been proud.

12 Rome and the Roman Empire: Background

The city of Rome came to prominence in Italy in the sixth century BC. It was a republic, governed by senate and consuls and with a citizen-army. As its power in Italy eventually grew, the city came into conflict with the great north African city of Carthage. Despite its redoubtable General Hannibal, Carthage was forced to sue for peace in 202BC after the battle of Zama. As the Roman Empire expanded into Greece, Macedonia, north Africa, Syria, Palestine and Egypt, the Romans felt able to call the Mediterranean *mare nostrum* - our sea.

Success abroad was not always reflected in peace in Rome. Power struggles developed between the two main political institutions, the Senate (dominated by the nobility) and the Assembly (representing the other citizens). From this conflict, ruthless army leaders could benefit. Julius Caesar's decision in 44BC to mint coins bearing his head appeared to be a clear statement of intent - he wanted to abolish the republic and rule as King. His death at the hands of senators led by Brutus and Cassius simply paved the way for more civil war. The triumph of Octavian (who adopted the name Augustus) heralded the end of the republic and the coming of the Empire (27BC).

13 Polybius (c. 200-c. 118BC): Background

Polybius was a Greek military leader (a cavalry commander) and statesman with no choice but to reflect on the faded power of Greece and the extraordinary dominance and power of the Roman Empire. This power had been brought home to him all too clearly when the Romans objected to the failure of Greeks like Polybius to support Rome in war against Macedonia. Polybius was one of a thousand Achaeans who were forced to live in exile in Italy from 167BC. However, he was permitted to live in Rome, where his relationship as friend and tutor to future senator Scipio Aemilianus brought him into intimate contact with the workings of the Roman political and social élites. It was 150BC before the surviving Achaeans were allowed to return home, but Polybius was far too useful for Rome to leave him in retirement. He was called to assist in war with Carthage, and took the opportunity to explore the African coast on board a ship placed at his disposal by Scipio. Unsurprisingly, all these experiences left their mark on his history.

14 The *Histories* of Polybius

There is a problem in dating the writing of the *Histories*. The work is divided into 40 books, and he probably wrote the final ten of them (which cover the period 167-146BC) towards the end of his life when he had returned from exile. So, the entire work was most certainly not written at one time: he clearly changed his mind at one point and decided to extend his account to 146BC (when he was present at the fall of Carthage). It is possible that the books appeared in stages, which would certainly help make his work topical. Walbank[9] suggests that this would suit Polybius' purpose in writing his history - to explain to his fellow Greeks what made the Romans so successful. This is what Polybius had to say about his purpose:

1   I am aware that some will be at a loss to account for my interrupting
     the course of my narrative for the sake of entering upon the following
     disquisition on the Roman constitution. But I think that I have already
     in many passages made it fully evident that this particular branch of my
5   work was one of the necessities imposed on me by the nature of my
     original design; and I pointed this out with special clearness in the
     preface which explained the scope of my history. I there stated that the
     feature of my work which was at once the best in itself, and the most
     instructive to the students of it, was that it would enable them to know
10   and fully realise in what manner, and under what kind of constitution,
     it came about that nearly the whole world fell under the power of
     Rome in somewhat less than fifty-three years, - an event certainly

without precedent. This being my settled purpose, I could see no more fitting period than the present for making a pause, and examining the
15 truth of the remarks about to be made on this constitution ... What is really educational and beneficial to students of history is the clear view of the causes of events, and the consequent power of choosing the better policy in a particular case. Now in every practical undertaking by a state we must regard as the powerful agent for success or failure
20 the form of its constitution; for from this as from a fountain-head all conceptions and plans of action not only proceed, but attain their consummation ...

Now the natural laws which regulate the merging of one form of government into another are perhaps discussed with greater accuracy
25 by Plato and some other philosophers. But their treatment, from its intricacy and exhaustiveness, is only within the capacity of a few. I will therefore endeavour to give a summary of the subject, just so far as I suppose it to fall within the scope of a practical history and the intelligence of ordinary people.

So, we have here an historian who clearly wished to make history practical, in the particular sense of being useful in military and political affairs. There are two main elements to this. First, it is vital to understand causation; second, the Roman constitution - its form of government - must be studied in order to understand what made it successful. And Polybius was keen to adapt the work of philosophers on this issue to make it more accessible and useful to ordinary people. By ordinary people he meant those who actually wielded political power. The implication behind his words, of course, is that he was writing more for Greeks than for Romans.

15 Polybius' Subject-Matter and Sources

Given his aims, it is hardly surprising that Polybius should have written near-contemporary and contemporary history or that he should have concentrated on diplomatic, political and military history in the manner of Thucydides. He did, however, allow himself some lengthy asides; particularly in his later books, where he was keen to exploit his sea-borne adventures and display his geographical knowledge. He was also keen to remind his readers that he was a man of action and not a desk-bound scholar, and he had some waspish things to say about other writers of histories for supposedly spending their time pouring over written sources in a library rather than getting to grips with the most important source - the eyewitness. It is not that Polybius failed to use written sources himself, but, in the manner of Thucydides, they are not discussed or identified as a matter of course. In book 12, he offered something new in historiography: what Walbank calls a 'systematic exposition of the methods to be used'[10]. Specifically, Polybius commented that history has three constituent parts: the collection and study of written sources, the survey of geographical locations; and finally - and most importantly for contemporary history - political experience. By this, he meant not so much actual participation in the events described as the ability to interview eyewitnesses and to put their evidence into the appropriate political and military context. His exile in Rome gave him a wonderful opportunity to conduct probing interviews, and there is every reason to believe that he kept notes of these for future use.

His subject-matter inevitably reflected those areas where he felt he had most expertise. He offered lengthy assessments of specific campaigns, commenting knowledgeably on the personal qualities of the generals, the use of cavalry and, in particular, what one could learn from the Roman successes. There were moral lessons to be learned about how men react to challenge and adversity. But of course it was the discussion of the Roman constitution which was fundamental to his aim of accounting for the triumph of Rome:

1　Now, it is undoubtedly the case that most of those who profess to give us authoritative instruction on this subject [types of constitution] distinguish three kinds of constitutions, which they designate *kingship, aristocracy, democracy* ... it is plain that we must regard as the *best* constitution
5　that which partakes of all these three elements.

Polybius also commented:

1　... there is a regular cycle of constitutional revolutions, and the natural order in which the constitutions change are transformed, and return again to their original stage. If a man have a clear grasp of these principles he may perhaps make a mistake as to the dates at which this or that
5　will happen to a particular constitution; but he will rarely be entirely mistaken as to the stage of growth or decay at which it has arrived, or as to the point at which it will undergo some revolutionary change ...
　　For the present I will make a brief reference to the legislation of Lycurgus ... That statesman was fully aware that all those changes which
10　I have enumerated come about by an undeviating law of nature; and reflected that every form of government that was unmixed, and rested on one species of power, was unstable; because it was swiftly perverted into that particular form of evil peculiar to it ... in kingship it is absolutism; in aristocracy it is oligarchy; in democracy lawless ferocity and
15　violence; and to these vicious states all these forms of government are ... inevitably transformed. Lycurgus, I say, saw all this, and accordingly combined together all the excellences and distinctive features of the best constitutions, that no part should become unduly predominant ... The result of this combination has been that the Lacedaemonians
20　retained their freedom for the longest period of any people with which we are acquainted ... the Romans have arrived at the same result in framing their commonwealth ...

This is unlike anything in Herodotus and goes far beyond any of

Thucydides' comments on political forms. At first sight, we have an impressive piece of political theorising in which the author claimed to have identified from his knowledge of history, politics and philosophy a kind of natural law or pattern in the past, present and future. Clearly, Polybius expected this to be of great value to those involved in political life. His concept of the virtues of the mixed constitution perhaps sits a little uneasily with the cycle of growth and decay, although, as we have seen, he did argue that the combination of elements of the three types of political system would evade the process. What this undeniably interesting model lacks, perhaps, is a sense of the subtleties of politics and the impact of individuals. Describing a constitution is one thing: understanding the people who work within it is another. Despite the time he spent in Rome, Polybius seems to have lacked the feel for the corridors of power and the less formal human interactions which shape the actual workings of government. Nor did his Greek mind-set help him much. As Momigliano points out, he tended to read Rome as a Greek city-state (hence his comparison of Sparta's constitution with that of Rome) and ignored some of the vital elements in the success of the Empire: namely, the way in which the aristocracy throughout Italy had been able to co-operate in imperial ventures. Polybius' treatment of Roman religion was similar to his treatment of Roman government. We get an acute and stimulating generalisation, but with something of an incon-sistency at its heart and a distinct lack of any sense of an individual's beliefs. He argued that the Roman authorities encouraged the ordi-nary people's 'scrupulous fear of the gods' as a way of keeping them well-behaved and in control for fear of punishment in the after-life. But if this was so, why did the very political élites who deliberately - and presumably cynically - exploited this fear apparently share it themselves?

> ... the Romans, in their magistracies and embassies ... have the handling of a great amount of money, and yet from pure respect to their oath keep their faith intact.

This extract might give the impression that Polybius' stance on the gods, at least, was straightforward enough. He claimed not to believe in them, but calmly suggested that encouraging the belief in others is invaluable for social and political stability. However, there is some-thing of an ambiguity in his attitude. He had a tendency to offer a dual explanation of some events: a rational assessment of causes and then a comment which implied - rather than clearly stated - an accep-tance of Fortune or Destiny. Rome's rise could be attributed to its constitution, yes; but there was also the sense in which that rise was presented as the workings of Fate. In fact, even where his analysis of causation was rational, it was often superficial. Possible underlying and long-term causes were ignored in favour of a shallow analysis of the motivation of those (usually from one side only) who were supposedly responsible for the outbreak of the conflict. Peter Derow, in his distinctly enthusiastic discussion of Polybius' qualities, admits that this kind of approach to causation is inadequate:

> Polybius is explaining ... nothing so general as why a war broke out, but more precisely why whoever began it began it ...[11]

16 Polybius and Speeches

Thucydides proclaimed that the speeches in his history were written to reflect what the occasion demanded that the speaker said, with due regard (wherever possible) to the actual words spoken. This rather elastic claim to accuracy and truth was stretched beyond the breaking point by many of his successors, who, as Walbank puts it, 'dropped all pretence of giving the real words'.[12] They simply used speeches as an opportunity to display their literary style. Polybius was clearly infuriated by this, and demanded that the historian should do as he did: relay to the best of his ability the actual words spoken. Given the importance he attached to eyewitnesses, it is hardly surprising that he should make this demand. But it would be even more surprising if he had consistently stuck to it himself. There are occasions - particularly in times of battle - where such claims are very unconvincing. He did admit at one point that he was following a common structure and even using the same words in some speeches. Perhaps the best assessment we can make is that he did the best he could to base his speeches on the actual recollection of eyewitnesses - particularly when the speakers were Greek.

17 Polybius' Contribution to Historiography

Polybius acknowledged no direct debt to Thucydides, but the latter's focus on political history remained. And it was Polybius, rather than Thucydides, who influenced the great historians of Rome - Livy, Sallust and Tacitus - to write political history with appropriate political (and moral) lessons. Polybius argued that ordinary men were transformed by the study of history into leaders, natural leaders were stimulated to be great by heroic examples and the wicked deterred by the fear of being held up to ridicule and shame.

A similar pattern can be detected in the Renaissance. His story of Rome was certainly more appealing to Renaissance scholars than Thucydides on the remoter war between Athens and Sparta. The Florentine scholar and politician Leonardo Bruni, for example, did much to establish Polybius as the model for good - and politically useful - history. His concept of the mixed constitution appealed directly to writers interested in the relationship between history and political theory, like Machiavelli (see page 44) and, later, Montesquieu (see page 51).

18 Roman Historiography

Roman historiography was by no means a mere imitation of a few Greek historians. It had its own native element in the brief summaries of public events (the *tabulae pontificum*) provided by the chief priests. Dominating it, however, were two crucial elements: the Roman sense of the political uses to which language could and should be put, and the view that it was right and proper to judge political behaviour in moral terms. So, it was hardly surprising that the Romans were most influenced by the Greek historians whose work seemed to reflect those demands. Or perhaps 'influenced' is an inadequate word to use. We should say that the Romans were selectively interested in their Greek predecessors where they found their approach, subject-matter and style to their taste.

Our starting point should be the work *De Oratore* (On the Orator) by the Roman writer Cicero (written c. 55BC), because Cicero's view of the relationship between history and rhetoric was enormously influential on Roman and Renaissance historiography. He complained that Roman historians were too often merely chroniclers of facts (on the model of the *tabulae pontificum*). What was needed was the use of rhetoric to elaborate on the dry and dull skeleton of fact. Classical rhetoric was, as Roger Ray puts it, 'primarily a theory of invention ... Indeed Aristotle defined the *entire* field of rhetoric as the faculty of finding (inventing) the means of persuasion on any subject whatever'.[13] Cicero's invention (*inventio*) means the devising of material which would make a case convincing. *Inventio* and history do not fit well together if one assumes that history must present what actually happened. The rhetorical historian was interested in the pursuit of truth, but this was not the truth dictated by events or the sources: it was the moral or political truth which his history had to serve. This meant that the historian had to be judgemental. Praise, blame and a style to arouse strong feelings were vital weapons to persuade the reader to imitate or to shun the behaviour of the historian's characters. Through his mouth-piece Antonius, Cicero said:

> And as History, which bears witness to the passing of the ages, sheds light upon reality, gives life to recollection and guidance to human existence, and brings tidings of ancient days, whose voice, but the orator's, can entrust her to immortality?

Rhetoric was much more than a call to use emotive language to persuade and inspire. In speeches - the obvious place for the rhetorical flourish - it involved a precise and formal structure, including methods for capturing the attention and goodwill of the listener, and a statement of facts, proof and conclusion.

19 Livy (Titus Livius) (c. 64BC-c. AD17)

Rhetoric can be seen hard at work in Livy's *The History of Rome from its Foundation*. It was much in evidence in the direct speeches provided by Livy in the smooth and flowing style recommended by Cicero in Book II of *De Oratore*. And Livy certainly set out to persuade:

I The study of history is the best medicine for a sick mind; for in history
  you have a record of the infinite variety of human experience plainly set
  out for all to see; and in that record you can find for yourself and your
  country both examples and warnings; fine things to take as models, base
5 things, rotten through and through, to avoid.
      I hope my passion for Rome's past has not impaired my judgment; for
  I do honestly believe that no country has ever been greater or purer
  than ours or richer in good citizens and noble deeds ...

So, we get a patriotic picture of the glory and might of Rome. Livy's reference to 'sick mind' reflected his attitude to the troubled times in which he was writing: probably the mid-30s BC, when Rome was embroiled in a civil war between Mark Anthony and the future Emperor Augustus. History, then, was to act as a moral and political tutor, needed more than ever when times were darkest. Livy's tales of the twins Romulus and Remus and the founding of Rome made a wonderful and intentionally inspiring story, while heroes like Hercules had their part to play in the early days of Rome. So did the gods. Livy did not hesitate to accept the involvement of the gods in human affairs. The Roman King Tullus Hostilius, for example, died in his burning palace after offending Jupiter Elicius by an unintentional mistake made in performing his rites to the singularly bad-tempered and vengeful god.

Livy set himself a monumental task in writing his great work. He intended to cover a period of some 800 years, and actually lived long enough to see something of the greatness of Rome revive under Augustus. Sadly, only the earlier volumes survive. Even so, we know that his undeniable skills of dramatic story-telling and unrepentant patriotism made his work extremely popular. But it seems a long way from the taut prose of the ex-soldier Thucydides to the elegance of Livy, the man of letters. Not for Livy was the Thucydidean expression of concern with the nature of historical sources: what mattered was the rhetorical impact on the reader.

20 Conclusions on Classical Historiography

Denys Hay rounds off a brief chapter on Greek and Roman historians in his book *Annalists and Historians* with a timely reminder which he then, it seems, proceeds to ignore:

> ... a word of warning should be addressed to those who did not heed
> the initial remark that classical historians were not trying to do what
> modern historians aim for.

But he adds:

> 1 ... it is salutary to remember how feeble was the tradition of ancient
> historiography. The three Greek authors mentioned [Herodotus,
> Thucydides and Polybius] had considerable merit. The Latins were a
> poor lot and it was the Latin writers rather than the Greeks who were
> 5 to have the largest influence in the centuries ahead, indeed almost to
> our own day.[14]

In my introduction, I suggested a set of criteria to help us to identify
the aims and characteristics of historians. I wanted as far as possible to
avoid the kind of judgement Hay appears to be making. Criticism can
avoid anachronism if every attempt is made to assess the historians on
their own terms. It is impossible to imagine an historian winning
much credibility today if he or she attempted to employ rhetoric to
teach a moral or political lesson, or perhaps made up speeches to
encompass those aims. By the same token, our objections would have
made little sense to Livy or Polybius. Nor would a modern definition
of historical truth which emphasises objectivity and perhaps neutrality
impress an historian for whom history was to serve truth, rather than
claim it for itself. To most classical historians, a work of history was a
fusion between the real and what could be passed off as real - all in the
service of truth. We cannot complain because this is not 'history as it
really happened', which is the tradition many of today's historians
were taught to accept as truth (along with the disciplined study of the
archive sources which gives history its voice). But what we can do is to
identify if and when a Greek or Roman historian failed to match his
own claims. This is why it is valid to complain if Herodotus was a little
too inclined to come up with convenient corroboration, or that
Polybius' speeches were unlikely to be as accurate as he claimed.

   The general themes of classical historiography are these.
Herodotus made inquiry into the past a valid enterprise and stimulated his successors to react to his approaches. He offered explanations which, superficially, appeared to attribute events to the activities
of the gods, but which in practice owed more to families and factions
tied into a web of obligation and revenge, often expressed as the
workings of fate. Thucydides replaced the Herodotean sense of
wonder and excitement with a cooler rationality which focused more
narrowly on military and political history and which rejected the
myths and legends his predecessor had both enjoyed and employed.
Neither Herodotus nor Thucydides offered explanations for events
which reflected the social and economic factors which were part of
the structures of society itself. Polybius, on the other hand, offered an
explanation of causation which blended (rather unsuccessfully) polit-

ical theory (the cyclical evolution of forms of government and the supposed benefits of a mixed constitution) with personal responsibility for great events: all rather mysteriously overlaid with vague references to fate and fortune. His history claimed to offer practical lessons in political and moral behaviour.

The assumption that history taught - and should be used to teach - moral and political lessons was subsequently treated to the intoxicating appeal of rhetoric. Cicero offered to Roman historians the technique to convince and persuade. Livy in particular made full use of it as he sought to inspire the reader to shun or more often to emulate the actions of the villains and heroes of his beloved Rome. Common to all classical historians was the view that the mentalities and world-view of individuals - and human nature itself - changed little throughout history. This is why the past could be used to teach by means of an analysis of a man's actions.

To say that the classical historians lacked a well developed technique for tackling and evaluating a range of historical sources is true enough. The emphasis placed on oral tradition or more particularly on oral contemporary history is entirely understandable - especially when we consider that the majority were political and military leaders themselves, and with valuable contacts to exploit. To blame or mock them for apparent limitations is another matter. We have no right to take them out of their time.

References

Please note that references are restricted to the secondary works mentioned in the text.

1   John Gould, *Herodotus* (Weidenfeld & Nicolson, 1989), p.17.
2   Detlev Fehling, *Herodotus and his 'Sources': Citation, Invention and Narrative Art* (Cairns, 1989).
3   Gould, *Herodotus*, p.41.
4   Peter Derow, in Simon Hornblower (ed.), *Greek Historiography* (Clarendon, 1994), p.76.
5   François Hartog, *The Mirror of Herodotus* (University of California Press, 1988), p.379.
6   Fehling, *Herodotus and his 'Sources'*, p.249.
7   Hornblower, *Greek Historiography*, p.79.
8   Arnaldo Momigliano, *The Classical Foundations of Modern Historiography* (University of California Press, 1990). See pp.44-5 in particular.
9   F.W. Walbank, *Polybius* (University of California Press, 1972).
10 Ibid., p.71.
11 Derow, in *Greek Historiography*, p.88.
12 Walbank, *Polybius*, p.44.
13 Roger Ray, in C. Holdsworth and T.P. Wiseman (eds.), *The Inheritance of Historiography 350-900* (University of Exeter Press, 1986), p.70.
14 Denys Hay, *Annalists and Historians: Western Historiography from the VIIIth to the XVIIIth Centuries* (Methuen, 1977), pp.10-11.

Making notes on 'The Birth of Historiography and the Historians of the Classical Period'

Some students assume that notes have to be committed to A4 lined paper, with lots of headings and sub-sections. There is nothing intrinsically wrong with this, but I would like to suggest an alternative (and tried and tested) method which lends itself very well to this chapter. Take a large sheet of paper (about the size of a single examination desk). Start in the top left hand corner with a spider diagram for Herodotus in the manner below. I have, of course, given you the basic structure for your notes in my criteria for evaluating historians. The great advantage of using this method of writing notes is that it allows for comparison of historians in a visually direct way (since they are all on one sheet of paper). It also forces you to make sense of the material: copying chunks out under the chapter's headings will not work.

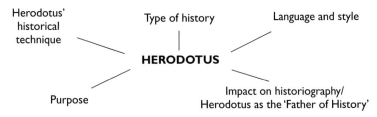

Now use the same approach for the other historians in the chapter.

Answering essay questions on 'The Birth of Historiography and the Historians of the Classical Period'

The most straightforward questions are those which demand an assessment of the qualities of a particular historian. In such essays, the five criteria described in section 1 can be used to provide a suitable structure. It is important to remember that examiners will expect you to refer to specific works by title and to demonstrate an awareness of the content of those works by use of detailed examples taken from them.

You might also be asked to compare the qualities of two or more historians. Once again, this is where the assessment criteria are so valuable. Candidates faced with a comparison question all too often write about the historians separately, only making direct comparisons in the conclusion. This means that little time is spent answering the question directly. It is much better to tackle the question thematically, using the five criteria as your main paragraph points. In this way, your whole essay will be devoted to direct comparisons. It is when answering such questions that notes made under the headings of the five criteria will prove to be very helpful.

Bear in mind the advice given above when preparing plans for the

following questions.
1. Compare Herodotus and Thucydides as historians.
2. 'The historian's most important quality is accuracy'. Discuss this view, with reference to any two historians writing in the Classical period.

Question 2 is full of potential danger, although the familiar strategy of identifying key-words should prevent you from making the disastrous mistake of assuming that it is solely about accuracy. It is vital to recognise that the question is actually about qualities in general, and that you will need to discuss a range of them, although you will be expected to spend more time on 'accuracy' than on any other. Remember that you will need to define each of the qualities you include.

It is also possible to get questions on the impact of a specific historian or historians on the study of history/historiography. These are more tricky. Such questions usually offer a choice of historians, and my advice would be to avoid choosing the Greeks or Romans. Far better to tackle those whose contributions are, to be frank, more direct and clear-cut, such as von Ranke (see pages 58-74) or the *Annales* school (pages 95-104).

Source-based questions on 'The birth of Historiography and the Historians of the Classical Period'

Carefully study the extracts from Thucydides on pages 14 and 15 and answer the following questions.
a) According to Thucydides, what were his purposes in writing his history? (4 marks)
b) What comments made by Thucydides suggest that his work is likely to be accurate? (6 marks)
c) What doubts might one have over Thucydides' accuracy? (4 marks)
d) What are the similarities and differences when one compares the subject-matter, language and style of Herodotus and Thucydides? (6 marks)

It is vital that, in answering source-based questions, you 'prove' your point by referring explicitly to the text - preferably by means of a brief quotation. Make the point first, then provide your quotation and, if possible, develop your argument further. Remember that examiners do not care for points without textual reference, and dislike equally an answer which tries to make the text do the work without a meaningful comment.

2 Christian Historiography

1 The Fall of the Roman Empire and the Growth of Christian Historiography

It was very tempting for a writer contemplating the might of Rome to assume that its Empire was eternal. It was, of course, no such thing. In the later fourth century AD, the Empire was battered by the movement of Germanic tribes, themselves being forced from their traditional lands by pressure from the East in the form of the nomadic Huns. Franks, Alemanni, Vandals, Visigoths, and Ostrogoths (all Germanic tribes) broke down the imperial borders. In AD 410, the Visigoth King Alaric took Rome itself. By AD 451, the Huns themselves were in Italy. The last Emperor in Rome, Romulus Augustulus, was dethroned by Odoacer in AD 476. This was the end of the western Empire based on Rome, although the eastern Empire based on Byzantium (created a joint capital by Emperor Constantine in AD 325) survived for another 1,000 years.

Britain, that far-flung outpost of the Empire, was similarly under threat, not only from the Germanic tribes, but also from its traditional enemies such as the Picts who lived in the north of the island, beyond Hadrian's Wall. Following the withdrawal of Roman troops from Britain, there seems to have been a gradual deterioration of Roman-style civil and military institutions and (as far as we can tell from archaeological evidence) in economic life as well. The situation was further complicated by accusations of heresy amongst British Christians, which led to the dispatch of the Bishop of Auxerre, Germanus, and the Bishop of Troyes, Lupus, to Britain in 429 with orders to quell it. Significantly, Germanus did not only provide religious assistance: as a former Roman general, he also found himself leading British forces to victory over an army of the old and new enemies - Picts and Saxons. But the future lay with the pagan Saxons. In fact, such Germanic tribes had already established areas of settlement in Britain before the collapse of Roman authority, but invitations - probably from Vortigern, a dominant figure in Britain from c. 425 to c. 450 and an opponent both of Rome and Germanus - brought in many more. By 500, Saxons and others were in control of areas of the eastern and south-eastern coasts - Kent, Sussex, Essex, East Anglia, East Yorkshire. By the middle of the seventh century, great Anglo-Saxon kingdoms had been established over much of England and southern Scotland.

This brief summary provides us with two main themes for examination: the collapse of the Roman Empire and the development of Christianity. What effect did these have on historiography?

Firstly, Christian historians found aspects of classical historiography impossible to accept. God, they argued, had a design for the world which was expressed through linear time. A cyclical pattern such as that proposed by Polybius could not be accepted, because they believed history began with the creation of Adam and would come to an end with Christ's Second Coming. And, since history contained the divine plan, it should be universal: an historical work should place its own particular subject within a survey of the whole of human history. This explains why medieval writers frequently felt the need to start their works with summaries of the main events from the Creation onwards - usually in the pattern of six ages identified by St Augustine in the early fifth century. The six ages corresponded with the account in the first chapters of Genesis of God's creation of the world in six days. To Augustine, the world had entered its sixth age with the coming of Christ. And then, when Christ returned - the Second Coming - the seventh age would herald the end of the world, and therefore of history itself.

Secondly, there was the issue of the Christians' attitude to the Roman Empire. It was difficult for them to view it positively while its emperors like Nero and Diocletian were persecuting Christians. But when, in 313, Emperor Constantine allowed Christians freedom of worship and subsequently gave Christianity the status of the official religion of the Empire, it became possible to see Rome as part of the divine plan. This attitude is at the heart of the *Ecclesiastical History* of Eusebius, Bishop of Caesarea and adviser to Constantine. Eusebius came to believe that the Church and the Empire were tied together intimately. This belief, of course, was difficult to sustain when the Empire fell in ruins. St Augustine, for example, in his *City of God* (written between 413 and 426) drew a distinction between the City of God and any earthly institution: it was therefore dangerous to claim a divine purpose for any empire or kingdom. Even so, some historians found it difficult to let the eternal Empire go. Augustine's follower Orosius, in his work *The Seven Books of the History against the Pagans*, saw the Empire as sanctified by its adoption of Christianity. He also took the opportunity to attack the pagans who argued that the Empire was collapsing as a result of becoming Christian.

Christian history was inevitably propagandist. We can take this word both in the modern sense of 'trying to persuade, usually by appealing to emotions and instincts' and in its original meaning of 'propagating the truth of faith'. History was an important weapon in the centuries during which Christianity had to oppose paganism. After all, it could be used to demonstrate the workings of God's plan through time. The arbitrary behaviour of gods or fate was replaced by the justice of God. Sin - often the sins of an entire people - therefore became an explanation of great events.

And finally, classical historians, as we have seen, generally preferred oral tradition or eyewitness account to the written source. This was an uncomfortable approach for a Christian historian, since his faith was fed not by oral sources but a work of written history - the Old and New

Testaments of the Bible. It is significant that Eusebius, for example, should interrupt his narrative with lengthy extracts from documents to 'prove' his argument.

2 The Venerable Bede (c. 672-735)

I have decided to discuss the Anglo-Saxon writer Bede for a number of reasons. In the first place, it is preferable to focus in some detail on particular historians rather than offer a survey of the entire field. In Bede's case, he gives us the chance to follow up the problems and issues facing the Christian historian writing in the post-Roman world. The final reason - and I hope the reader will be prepared to accept that this is not uppermost in my mind - is because I find Bede and his age fascinating in their own right. As we shall see, he wrote with a splendid clarity and vigour which have a very special appeal.

Bede was a monk of the twin Northumbrian abbeys of Monkwearmouth and Jarrow. It is all too easy to imagine his home as isolated and lacking in cultural life, but this would be quite wrong. The seven Anglo-Saxon Kingdoms of England had close contacts with the Continent, and it was the Anglo-Saxon Church which sent missionaries to Europe in the late seventh century in an attempt to convert the many remaining pagans among the Saxons. The Church in Northumbria itself owed much to the Irish missionaries from Iona, and Bede's own monastery had a superb library courtesy of its founder in c. 681, Benedict Biscop. The works by Eusebius and Orosius were among many available to Bede.

The European cultural links were reflected in Bede's contemporary popularity in Christian Europe. He was not seen primarily as an historian, but more as a scholar whose biblical commentaries were the most popular of his many works. It is significant that, as he was dying, he struggled to finish a work of biblical translation. The future abbot of Wearmouth and Jarrow, Cuthbert, reported:

> There was one of us with him who said: 'Beloved master, there is still one chapter missing from the book you were dictating, but it seems to me difficult to ask you for more.' But he answered: 'It is easy. Take your pen and prepare it and write quickly.' And this he did.

Bede's considerable output included chronicles of the world (in the sense of lists of dated events, based on Eusebius and his continuators). These lists were part of two works on chronology, *De Temporibus (Time)* and *De Tempore Ratione (The Reckoning of Time)* which, together with his historical writing, represent the first consistent attempt to date events using the Incarnation of Christ as the focal point. The dating systems of the classical historians was confusing and imprecise, and some Christian writers had attempted to introduce a system of dating by reference to Diocletian, the great persecutor of Christians. Bede's work spread the AD/BC system throughout Europe. He also wrote on the geography of the Holy Land and saints' lives (hagiography). His summarising of saints' lives in the order in which they appeared in the church's calendar was highly influential. He wrote lives of individual saints and works of science derived from classical writers. There is a central theme running through this impressive list, and that is Bede's view of himself as a teacher: or, more precisely, as a propagandist for his version of orthodox Christianity in a society which was by no means fully converted. On that death bed, he was not really dictating: to the last, he was teaching. It is important to bear this in mind in any assessment of his historical writings.

3 Bede's Use of Sources and Purpose

Historians who have little good to say of the classical historians or the Christian historians of the so-called Dark Ages generally raise their hats to Bede. It is easy to see why. His *Ecclesiastical History of the English People* - completed in c. 732 - had some things to say about methodology which sound sweet to modern ears. In his preface, Bede addressed King Ceolwulf of Northumbria, to whom the work is dedicated:

1   But in order to avoid any doubts in the mind of yourself, or of any who may listen to or read this history, as to the accuracy of what I have written, allow me briefly to state the authorities upon whom I chiefly depend. My principal authority and adviser in this work has been the

5   most reverend Abbot Albinus, an eminent scholar educated in the church of Canterbury by Archbishop Theodore and Abbot Hadrian, both of them respected and learned men. He carefully transmitted to me verbally or in writing through Nothelm, a priest of the church of London, anything he considered worthy of mention that had been done

10   by disciples of the blessed Pope Gregory in the province of Kent or the surrounding regions. Such facts he ascertained either from records or from the recollection of older men. Nothelm himself later visited Rome, and obtained permission from the present Pope Gregory to examine the archives of the holy Roman Church ... Also the most reverend

15   Bishop Daniel of the West Saxons, who is still alive, sent to me in writing certain facts about the history of the Church in his province ... I have learnt by careful enquiry from the brethren of Lastingham monastery how by the ministration of the holy priests Cedd and Chad, their founders, the faith of Christ came to the province of the Mercians ...

20   With regard to events in the various districts of the province of the Northumbrians, from the time that it received the Faith of Christ up to the present day, I am not dependent on any one author, but on countless faithful witnesses who either know or remember the facts, apart from what I know myself.

The historian Goffart enthusiastically comments:

> ... a mastery of historical technique incomparable for its time ... and, not least, an author whose qualities of life and spirit set a model of dedicated scholarship.[1]

We can see what Goffart means. Bede is naming many of his sources and types of information and not simply paying lip-service to the process. Antonia Gransden points out that he even instructed scribes to name authorities in the margins of his biblical commentaries. Like Eusebius, he copied documents directly into his text (many of which, of course, would have come from Nothelm's work in the Roman archives). Where Bede's sources were oral, he often named the informant. In book V, for instance, he wrote of miracles performed by John of Beverley and cited as his main source Berthun:

> ... a most reverend and truthful man, formerly John's deacon and now abbot of the monastery known as In-Derawuda ...

So, we are given not only the name and a comment on his likely truthfulness, but also the relationship between the informant and John. We also discover the informant's whereabouts. It was by no means unknown for medieval writers to come up with a fictitious informant, but the detail here is too extensive (and verifiable by Bede's readership) for it to be likely in this case.

Despite - or rather because of - these praise-worthy and rigorous attempts to uncover the truth, Bede was, it seems, only too willing to admit his fallibility:

> 1 Should the reader discover any inaccuracies in what I have written, I humbly beg that he will not impute them to me, because, as a true law of history requires, I have laboured honestly to transmit whatever I could ascertain from common report for the instruction of posterity.
>
> 5   I earnestly request all who may hear or read this history of our nation to ask God's mercy on my many failings of mind and body.

The historian Dahmus comments that this statement marks Bede as a 'true historian'.[2]

However, in *An English Empire*, Higham presents a very different view of Bede.

> Bede could be, and often was, mischievous. He was also writing within a particular literary and intellectual environment so far distant from our own that it is a risky business to describe him by such words as 'historian' at all.[3]

Given what I have already said about the dangers of anachronistic judgement, you will see that I am likely to welcome Higham's reminder about the need to root an evaluation of Bede in his own time. His charge is that Bede is not the detached scholar, remote from the world, seeking to employ a methodology which allows him to recover the past without the distortion of his own political circumstances. And much of Higham's charge, I believe, sticks.

Our first point concerns Bede's apparent readiness to admit his own errors and failings. Higham sees this as an essentially literary device known as *sermo humilis* ('humble words' or 'humble sermon') rather than something personal to Bede. In any case, as we shall see, Bede is more than ready to make sweeping judgements without a trace of that humility. And secondly, we have to consider Bede's purpose. As we have already seen, he spoke of his work as being written for the 'instruction of posterity'. This sounds like many a classical historian, but Bede was not writing an openly political manual. His work had an evangelical purpose - to spread the correct teaching of Christ's gospel, as distilled by the Roman Church and the contemporary needs of his own Northumbrian Church. A detached and objective historian he was not. After all, it is not likely that Bede would be somehow remote from his Anglo-Saxon political environment. He was a Northumbrian, proud of his Northumbrian Kingdom of Bernicia: and this, too, distorted his work.

It is hardly surprising that Bede should have a polemical purpose in his history. We recall that he saw himself primarily as a teacher with the most important message of all: the true faith of Christ. He shared this with his predecessors Eusebius (as translated into Latin and extended by Rufinus), Orosius and Gildas. The latter's mid sixth-century work *The Ruin of Britain* dealt with the end of Roman Britain and the Anglo-Saxon invasions by blaming them all on the sins of the Britons. With all these authors, Bede shared the view that God's providence was working through history.

The workings of God were charted by Bede in a number of ways. The most obvious is the frequent references to miracles: a superb teaching aid, of course, to reveal to the pagan and faithful alike the power of God. Some of the miracles are particularly dramatic and defy every natural law. In book IV, we have a wonderful (in every sense) tale of a young warrior, Imma, who was wounded in battle and imprisoned. But no chains could be made to stay on him, and this was because his brother, thinking him dead, was having prayers said for his soul. Similarly, when pagan Old Saxons in Germany martyred two English missionaries - the Hewald brothers - and threw them into the Rhine, their bodies were carried *upstream* nearly 40 miles and with appropriate lighting effects courtesy of a spectacular thunderstorm. Bede also included the tale of the eyes of St Alban's executioner, which dropped out as he struck the fatal blow. This is not to say that the *Ecclesiastical History* is simply a list of spectacular miracles. Some of the miracles seem a little more mundane, in that God did not always suspend the workings of nature. Dangerous fires are blown out through prayer, but also through a natural occurrence such as a change in wind-direction or a sudden calm. And Bede did make some effort to name his witnesses for the miracles where possible. The hermit Ethelwald's miraculous calming of a storm was witnessed by:

> one of the brethren among whom and for whose benefit it was performed; this was the venerable priest and servant of Christ Guthfrid, who afterwards presided as abbot over the brethren of the church of Lindisfarne where he had been brought up.

Miracles of whatever type have the necessary persuasive power, and Bede was keen to make the point that God intervened directly in the world to reward virtue and to punish sin. He stressed the workings of the hand of God in the affairs of kings, whose role was to serve and protect the church. Gransden sums this up conveniently:

> ... God rewarded good kings with victory and prosperity, and punished bad ones with earthly calamities.[4]

Bede's comments on King Edwin of Northumbria are a case in point.

> As a sign that he would come to the Faith and the heavenly kingdom, King Edwin received wide additions to his earthly realm.

This highly propagandist style of history is bound to lead to distortion. It would, for example, be very difficult for Bede to admit to the successes of pagan kings. In book II, we have a list of kings with lordship (known later as Britain-rulers or 'Bretwaldas') over much of England - and he missed out two who just happened to be pagans. Similarly, he took from Gildas the view that the Anglo-Saxon invasions had been a punishment from God for the sins of the British. His attitude to the Britons was also unreasonably harsh for religious reasons.

Bede's deeply-felt loyalty to the Pope meant that he was angrily unfair to the Church of the Britons - particularly those Christians in Wales who, at the time he was writing, would accept neither the authority of English bishops nor Roman practices, such as the method of dating Easter. In book II, he described the attempts made by Augustine to persuade them to conform. They stubbornly refused, despite a miracle performed by him for their benefit. Augustine offered a compromise: if they would abide by the dating of Easter, conduct the sacrament of baptism properly and - significantly - preach the gospel to the English, then their other unique practices could be maintained. Still they refused, and Bede claimed that the monks of Bangor were put to the sword by the pagan King Ethelfrid as punishment from God. Ethelfrid was King of Bernicia - a consideration which may have helped Bede in making a pagan the instrument of God.

There is the hint here that we would be wrong to see Bede's distortions as purely religious. In an era where Church and State were bound up in the most intimate of ties, Bede was in no position, even if he had wanted to, to isolate himself from secular (worldly) considerations. There is no sign that he wanted to. Bede was every inch a Northumbrian and every millimetre a Bernician, and so he wrote his history with the contemporary political situation very much in mind.

Higham's discussion of this issue is most helpful. He argues convincingly that Bede responded to the contemporary dominance of Mercia over the Anglo-Saxon Kingdoms - a dominance fought over with Bernicia for a century - by downplaying the importance of Mercia and exaggerating the power of Bernicia in his work. The rightful claim to *imperium* - to the inheritance of the Roman domination of much of Britain - is handed over to Bernicia and denied to Mercia in a way which flies in the face of historical fact. When Bede felt the necessity to praise a Mercian king, he made sure that Bernicia was not overshadowed. In book V, we have the example of Coenred, King of Mercia, who resigns his throne and leaves for Rome to become a monk. His departure is dated not according to his own years on the throne, but according to the fourth year of the *imperium* of the eight-year old King of Northumbria. We are then treated not to an account of his stay in Rome, but to a very lengthy description of the death and career of the Northumbrian Bishop Wilfrid. It is not that Bede failed to praise Coenred - he did - but that his attention was clearly elsewhere. Even the Mercian Church gets little mention. We recall that, in the preface, Bede cited (named) his source for information on that church - the monastery of Lastingham. All well and good, one might think. But Lastingham was not in Mercia. It was, needless to say, in Northumbria.

So, the picture we are getting of Bede is not that of the unworldly scholar, unaffected by and uninterested in the secular world lapping at the doors of his haven. Instead, we have a picture of a man who was very much of his time. His evangelical zeal and his love for Bernicia were hardly likely to be cast aside when he picked up his pen. In fact, they complemented each other. As Gransden points out, Bede looked at the reign of King Edwin (616-632) as a golden age for Northumbria in both secular and spiritual terms. He wanted that age to come again, and wrote his history with that aim in mind. One can see his priorities very clearly in his dedication of the *Ecclesiastical History*, not to a bishop or abbot, but to the Northumbrian king, Ceolwulf.

4 Bede, Style and Rhetoric

It is a commonplace - but none the less true for that - that Bede was an excellent stylist. He wrote with impressive clarity, and could describe with admirable vigour and without pretension. But this is a minor point. What really matters is to consider the question of whether Bede sought to use the tools of classical rhetoric in his desire to evangelise and persuade. After all, as we saw in Chapter 1, rhetoric was a device which sought to persuade the audience or readership of a particular moral or political truth. The accurate recording of the past was less important in itself than that truth. According to Roger Ray, he did use rhetoric to evangelise and persuade. After all, Bede made use of writers like Orosius and Eusebius who were certainly familiar with rhetoric. Ray believes that Bede knew something of Cicero's work. However, the strongest part of Ray's case is when he looks in detail at what Bede had to say. There is a telling quotation from the preface, in which Bede describes the purpose of his history:

1 For if history records good things of good men, the thoughtful hearer is encouraged to imitate what is good: or if it records evil of wicked men, the devout, religious listener or reader is encouraged to avoid all that is sinful and perverse and to follow what he knows to be good
5 and pleasing to God.

Much of this could have come from the pen of Livy himself. Ray also believes that the geographical and ethnographical introduction after the preface bears the hallmarks of the rhetorical historian. But when we get to the debate at the Synod of Whitby, we see Bede adopting, not only the technical terminology of rhetoric, but also a pattern of paired speeches:

a favourite form of Roman deliberative oratory and a preferred device of rhetorical historians.[5]

This is not to suggest that Bede, like Livy, invented speeches as a matter of course. But one has to say that there are times when the sheer quality of his writing testifies to his desire to persuade more than it testifies to his concern for strict accuracy. Take this wonderful speech by a member of King Edwin's council as it deliberated the value of adopting the Christian faith:

1 Your Majesty, when we compare the present life of man on earth with that time of which we have no knowledge, it seems to me like the swift flight of a single sparrow through the banqueting-hall where you are sitting at dinner on a winter's day with your thegns and counsellors. In
5 the midst there is a comforting fire to warm the hall; outside, the storms of winter rain or snow are raging. This sparrow flies swiftly in through one door of the hall, and out through another. While he is inside, he is safe from the winter storms; but after a few moments of comfort, he vanishes from sight into the wintry world from which he came. Even so,
10 man appears on earth for a little while; but of what went before this life or of what follows, we know nothing. Therefore, if this new teaching has brought any more certain knowledge, it seems only right that we should follow it.

Persuaded by such eloquence, the Chief Priest rushed off to smash his pagan idols.

5 Conclusion on Bede

Antonia Gransden offers a suitably up-beat assessment of Bede which is well worth quoting at some length:

1   … the *Ecclesiastical History* owes its lasting reputation to Bede's ability
as an historian. His grasp of historical method was unique in the middle
ages. It appears in his chronology and in the competence with which he
collected data … Bede exploited all resources. He ransacked the library
5   and archives at Wearmouth/Jarrow, asked his friends to search for documents, and questioned people he met. Unlike most medieval writers he
meticulously named most of his sources of information, literary, documentary and oral.[6]

It was clearly important for Bede to name his authorities, and one can
see why. His history was propagandist: like Eusebius and Orosius, he
was out to persuade the pagan or to cement the faith of the Christian.
To do so, he sought to convince in a number of ways. Citing sources
was one, but so was - if we accept Ray's argument - the use of rhetoric.
So was the use of miracles, or the distortions whereby he aimed to
convince listeners (or readers) that Christians succeed both in this life
and in the life to come. The truth for Bede was not some sort of
neutrality marked by objectivity; nor was history a method of letting
the past speak for itself. It was the Christian truth, and in the truth of
history was God's plan revealed. Even then, Bede's particular version
of Christian historical truth was further coloured by his love of the
Church of Rome, Bernicia, Northumbria and Anglo-Saxon England -
very much in that order. He was not in a position to ignore secular
matters given the way in which Church and State were intertwined in
his society.

What were the links between Bede, his predecessors and his successors? Because Bede is something of a jewel among medieval historians, it is sometimes tempting to set him apart as if he was untouched
by the historiographical context. The influence of Orosius we
detected in his geographical introduction, and his chronologies
reflect the work of Eusebius. The influence of Cicero was more difficult to detect, but we pointed to rhetorical flourishes in his work.

We should also consider the relationship between the so-called
early medieval annal and Bede. Annals were essentially lists of events,
generally without a connecting narrative. The Christian version of
annals grew out of the Easter tables, which were drawn up in monastic
and other great churches to calculate the date of Easter: a moveable
feast and the greatest of the Christian festivals. From this date, one
could calculate the Paschal Term (the date of Passover) and write in
the other important days in the Church year. And, in the gaps, one
could write down news of any important events which the computist
(the calculator of the tables) thought of interest. Given that the
computist was almost always a monk, the events were often of significance to his own monastery, and references to national happenings
were rarely politically astute. Storms and sheep, yes - political analysis,
absolutely not. Perhaps because Bede's *Ecclesiastical History* is so relatively sophisticated and had involved extensive research, the standard

form of medieval historiography, the medieval chronicle, developed more out of the annals than it did out of Bede. There are other possible reasons why medieval historians did not, in general, write as the heirs of Bede. His miracle stories were much appreciated and enjoyed but, as society became more exclusively Christian, the evangelical purpose of Bede's anti-pagan stance became less appropriate. Against this, there are some medieval historians who clearly appreciated and sought to copy Bede's methods. The best examples are the twelfth-century chroniclers of England, Orderic Vitalis and William of Malmesbury.

6 Medieval Historiography

In this section I do not intend to cover the whole of medieval historiography, but instead will focus on two features which are typical of the approaches to history in the Middle Ages. First of all, I will look more closely at the annal, and will do so by using as an example the *Anglo-Saxon Chronicle*. We then need to examine the problems medieval historians had in identifying the difference between past and present.

The *Anglo-Saxon Chronicle* (or chronicles, as there are several versions reflecting different local interests) is unusual in being written in the vernacular (the native tongue) rather than in Latin. Its early versions are, however, typically annalistic. First started sometime in the reign of King Alfred (871-99), it began with the creation, offering brief factual statements year by year. Detail certainly increased from Alfred's reign onwards, but with little or nothing by way of a linked narrative. We can take an example to illustrate this from the entry for 891 AD:

> In this year, the host went east; and king Arnulf fought against the mounted host, before the ships came, with the East Franks and the Saxons and the Bavarians, and put it to flight.
>
> And three Irishmen came to king Alfred in a boat without any oars ... and Suibhne, the best teacher among the Scots, died ... And the same year after Easter ... appeared the star which in Latin is called 'cometa' ...

The standard of explanation is clearly poor, and information of all sorts is thrown together indiscriminately. Even the chronology was sometimes unreliable - partly because of copyists' mistakes, partly because it is not always clear on which day the particular chronicler started the new year.

The *Anglo-Saxon Chronicle* started to offer more by way of a linked narrative with the tenth-century Danish invasions, but the annalistic format inevitably hindered an effective analysis of causes. After all, how does one explore longer or medium-term causes when tied to a one-thing-after-another, year-by-year approach? And it was this framework that the *Chronicle* (which lasted into the twelfth century) left to subsequent chroniclers in England. Difficulty with handling sophisticated causation was not simply a characteristic of English medieval historiography. Historians throughout Christian Europe had the tendency to ascribe causes either to God's will or to a rather superficial account of personal motives. In any case, since many of the chroniclers were monks, their awareness of secular affairs was generally limited. The following comment by Orderic Vitalis was a little overstated, but not by much:

> Skilful historians could write a memorable history of these great men and women ... We, however, who have no experience of the courts of the world, but spend our lives in the daily rounds of the cloisters where we live, will briefly note what is relevant to our purpose.[7]

It was a characteristic of medieval society that change was so slow that it was almost undetectable. This meant that there were few examples where historians could actually see clear breaks between times in the past. The trap of anachronism therefore lay gaping, and most fell straight in without noticing the thud. The medieval writer (like his Greek predecessor) simply assumed that the structures of society and human behaviour were unchanging, and therefore foisted on the past his own attitudes and experience. This partly explains the widespread success of what we would call forgeries. Perhaps the best-known example is the spurious *Donation of Constantine* in which the Emperor is supposed to have granted Italy to the Pope as the latter's own territory. This forgery could be seen as authentic only if scholars failed to notice its obvious anachronisms because they lacked the sense of difference between present and past.

The frequent use of forgery - and many monasteries forged land deeds for property they genuinely felt but could not prove was theirs - is suggestive of a casual approach to historical evidence. It is unusual to find a medieval historian who balanced different types of evidence to make a judgement, and very usual to find him simply lifting evidence from other writers without any form of assessment or evaluation.

However, by the late thirteenth century the monastic chronicle appeared to be on the wane. I am reluctant to use an unhelpful phrase like 'the spirit of the age was changing', so perhaps I can suggest that the monastic life, with its assumption that the attitude of *contemptu mundi* - avoiding the snares of worldly life - was the best route to salvation, found itself increasingly challenged by the activities of the new orders of friars who worked with and in the secular world. Towns were growing, and, with an increasing lay readership, urban chronicles started to develop which were as interested in the doings of burghers and mayors as they were in the deeds of saints, bishops and kings. Here is an increasing openness to the world, and one which was evident in the period known as the Renaissance.

7 Renaissance Historiography

The word 'Renaissance' is an historian's construct, so it might be best to start with the Swiss scholar Jacob Burckhardt whose book of 1860, *The Civilisation of the Renaissance in Italy*, established a definition which has endured, even if only as a target at which modern historians can aim. The Renaissance, said Burckhardt, was indeed a 'new birth', represented by the

1   ... great and general enthusiasm of the Italians for classical antiquity [which] really begins in the fourteenth century. For this a development of civic life was required, which took place only in Italy, and there not till then: that noble and burgher live together on equal terms, but a society
5   arise which felt the need for culture, and had the leisure and the means to obtain it. But culture, as soon as it freed itself from the reverie of the Middle Ages, could not at once and without help find its way to understanding the physical and intellectual world. It needed a guide, and found one in the ancient civilisation, with its wealth of truth and knowledge in
10 every spiritual interest. Both the form and the substance of this civilisation were adopted with admiring gratitude; it became the chief part of the culture of the age.[8]

Most of Burckhardt's arguments have been exposed as over-generalisations, exaggerations or both. Medieval attitudes and traditions survived into the so-called Renaissance period; Burckhardt's dramatic contrast between Italy and the rest of Europe is similarly overplayed. There was more adaptation and less slavish imitation of classical models than he thought.

Even so, the Renaissance remains a meaningful label - in part because those involved in its wide-ranging cultural life believed that they were shaping something new. But the Renaissance label is not the only one we need to discuss. We have German historians of the nineteenth century to thank for 'humanism', although they in turn were adapting the fifteenth-century word *humanistae*, referring to teachers of *studia humanitatis*: grammar, rhetoric, poetry, ethics and history. For our purposes, its meaning is really two-fold: in its wider sense, it is a 'belief in the dignity and potential of man'; in its narrower sense, it means 'an interest in Greek and Latin literature, from which vital lessons for the improvement of the individual and society were to be drawn'. In this quest, history played a significant part. This is not to say that humanists adopted a non-Christian system of morality. The learning of the past could be used to help society to progress in its Christianity, not to become less Christian.

A sense of progress demands an awareness of change, and this represents one of the most important characteristics of Renaissance thought. The founding father of Renaissance humanism is traditionally seen as the Florentine scholar and poet Petrarch (1304-74), whose researches and antiquarian interests led him to an awareness of the distinction between the classical period and his more recent past. In one sonnet, he significantly referred to the glories of the past and to the lack of such glories in the middle age in which he lived:

1 Long before my birth time smiled and may again,
    for once there was, and yet will be, more joyful days.
    But in this middle age time's dregs
    sweep around us, and we bend beneath a heavy
5 load of vice. Genius, virtue, glory now
    have gone, leaving chance and sloth to rule.

The sense of the essential difference of the past - so foreign to the medieval chronicler - was subsequently reflected in many aspects of Renaissance culture. In painting and architecture, artists were criticised for anachronism. The architect Antonio Filarete insisted:

> If you have to do a thing that represents the present time, do not dress your figures in the antique fashion. In the same way, if you have to represent antiquity, do not dress them in modern dress.

This awareness of difference enabled scholars of philology (the study of language) to exploit a parallel awareness of style and the development of language to evaluate the authenticity of documents.

The humanist call, then, was for a return *ad fontes* - to the wellspring or sources of knowledge: in other words, to those who shaped and recorded the ancient world. In his enthusiasm, Petrarch wrote letters to his long-dead heroes Cicero and Livy, calling the latter 'thou matchless historian'.

It is hardly surprising that Renaissance historians should seek to model their history on their classical predecessors. One mark of this was the desire to write the history of one's city-state in the manner of Livy. A good example of this is Leonardo Bruni (c. 1374-1444), whose *History of the Florentine People* offers the typical classical justification for the study of history: it was to encourage virtue by offering examples to emulate (try to copy) or to shun. Bruni charted the rise of Florence, drawing parallels with that of ancient Rome, and invoked republican liberty as the great cause of Florence's eminence. He followed his masters in making up speeches, and wrote a Latin which was classical rather than late medieval. It is tempting to write off Bruni as merely derivative, but he transcended his Roman predecessors in the way in which he compared and evaluated his written sources. But Bruni stands out among a rather less worthy group of emulators of Livy and others who, over-dosing on Ciceronian rhetoric, produced weak imitations which distorted the history of their chosen cities. Felix Gilbert[9] charts the failings of Bernardo Rucellai, who tackled the Florence dominated by the charismatic friar and preacher Savonarola by ignoring Savonarola whenever possible, on the grounds that he did not fit conveniently the classical models.

It is a sign of the importance attached to humanist scholarship in the Italian city-states that good scholars could hope for influential political posts without necessarily having undergone an apprenticeship in administration or diplomacy. And the experience of the hazardous world of fifteenth and sixteenth-century Italian politics was in turn likely to exert a marked influence on those who subsequently wrote history. The best example is Niccolò Machiavelli (1469-1527), who was made second chancellor of the Florentine Republic in 1498 largely on the strength of his preparation in the *studia humanitatis*. His education and his diplomatic missions to France, where he met the ruthless and audacious Cesare Borgia, Duke of Romagna, and to the papal court, where he met the equally ruthless and audacious Pope Julius II, shaped his important works of history and politics: in particular, his *Discourses on Livy* (1513-21), his *Florentine Histories* (c. 1525) and *The Prince* (1516). The work on Livy reflected his acceptance of the standard classical assumption that the study of history was of great value to statesmen, and he therefore attempted to explore the history of Rome and to make use of Polybius' cyclical pattern of historical change to provide lessons for Florence itself. His *Florentine Histories* also made use of his observation of Borgia and Julius II in action. He came to admire the way in which they lied, deceived and acted ruthlessly whenever they needed to. Fortune, in Machiavelli's terms, clearly favoured the brave, and the man of virtue (*virtu*) who was to be emulated was more Cesare than Christ: manly, but also self-centred and amoral (without any moral sense). Writing up this kind of insight in the political manual *The Prince* meant that Machiavelli was distancing himself even from Roman moralists, for whom princely virtue meant honesty, wisdom and justice. He was also creating an unenviable reputation for himself as an amoral political thinker: hence the origin of the term 'Machiavellian', which means crafty, cunning and - of course - ruthless. It should, however, be emphasised that Machiavelli was most unusual in setting aside the Christian world-view and its moral teachings.

In any conclusion on the Renaissance historians, it is tempting to dismiss them as pale imitators of their classical heroes. As we have seen, some did distort everything they wrote to fit the antique model. Most were influenced by the Roman historians rather than Herodotus and Thucydides, and this was perhaps unfortunate. Nevertheless, there were those - like Machiavelli - who were less slavish and more inclined actually to make use of the insights and aims of the classical historians to reflect their own times and their own needs.

Clearly, the Renaissance sense of anachronism was a vital gift for the future. However, it has to be said that humanist historians, whilst recognising the difference between their present and their past, assumed that the world-view or mentality of those living in ancient Rome was little different from their own, and that human nature and behaviour did not fundamentally change through time. Such an assumption was, in fact, rarely challenged before the nineteenth century (see pages 57-59).

8 Conclusion

The Christian world-view had a fundamental impact on the writing of history. There are few direct links between classical and medieval historiography, because the world-view was profoundly different. The secular perspective of the classical period, where history had important political and moral lessons to teach, was replaced by a history in which the Christian God shaped every aspect of life. After all, the annal developed, not from a tradition of historical writing, but from the gaps left in Easter tables. The annalist frequently lacked a grasp of secular politics, but had a firm interest in the doings of the monastery in which he worked and in the way God manifested Himself in the dramas and tragedies of everyday life. The medieval writer, with his concept of the progress of time from creation to Second Coming, often felt the need to summarise history before his own day to locate himself within the divine plan. Bede's *Ecclesiastical History*, with its discussion of sources and historical technique, and its occasional use of the classical tradition of rhetoric, seems to stand alone in its sophistication. But we discovered that Bede in no way transcended his time. He wrote a work with an evangelical purpose: the remaining pagans should be converted and the Christians reassured that God would reward them on earth and in heaven. Bede's scholarly qualities found few imitators, and, as the threat of lingering paganism receded, so did the value of his historical work in the eyes of his successors.

Although it is frequently argued that the period of the so-called Renaissance did not represent as much of a break with the medieval past as was once thought, there are marked differences in much of the historiography. It became fashionable to disparage the medieval chroniclers and to praise their classical forebears. And so, despite a new awareness of the discontinuities of the past, there was some unthinking imitation of historians like Livy. In other cases, we noted an adapting of classical concepts such as *virtus* (the Latin form and origin of the Italian *virtu*) to reflect the political realities of the fifteenth and early sixteenth century. Whatever approach was taken, history was once more the teacher of statesmen.

References

1   Walter Goffart, *The Narrators of Barbarian History* (Princeton University Press, 1988), p. 235.

2   J.H. Dahmus, *Seven Medieval Historians* (Nelson-Hall, 1982), p. 48.

3   N.J. Higham, *An English Empire. Bede and the early Anglo-Saxon kings* (Manchester University Press, 1995), p. 9.

4   Antonia Gransden, *Historical Writing in England, c. 550-c.1307* (Routledge & Kegan Paul, 1974), p. 22.

5   Roger Ray, in C. Holdsworth and T.P. Wiseman (eds.), *The Inheritance of Historiography 350-900* (University of Essex Press, 1986), p. 80.

6   Gransden, *Historical Writing*, p. 25.

7 Orderic Vitalis, quoted in Beryl Smalley, *Historians in the Middle Ages* (Thames & Hudson, 1974), p. 88.
8 Jacob Burckhardt, *The Civilisation of the Renaissance in Italy* (Mentor, 1960), p. 148.
9 Felix Gilbert, *Machiavelli and Guicciardini* (Norton, 1965)

Making notes on 'Christian historiography'

Although the main focus of this chapter has been on Bede, it is important to understand the main features of medieval and Renaissance historiography. I suggest, therefore, that notes be made in the manner suggested on page 28, and that the summary diagram below be used for the layout and headings.

Summary Diagram
Christian Historiography

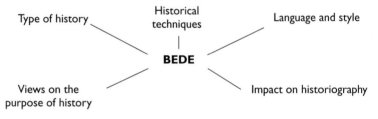

Differences between medieval and classical views on history and the purpose of historiography

Type of history — Historical techniques — Language and style

BEDE

Views on the purpose of history — Impact on historiography

Comparison between Bede and the main features of the Medieval annal

Definition of Renaissance and Humanism — Humanist criticism of 'Middle Ages'

RENAISSANCE HISTORIOGRAPHY
main characteristics

Attitude to human behaviour and nature — Imitation of classical historians — Machiavelli's uniqueness

Answering essay questions on 'Christian Historiography'

The types of question you will meet are likely to be very similar to those asked about classical historiography: namely, a focus on the qualities of a specified historian or the 'how good an historian is …' style. Therefore, the advice given on pages 28-29 is relevant to this topic also.

Try writing plans for the following:

1. 'Bede stands alone: by the standards of his time, he was an excellent historian.' Comment on this view.
2. 'Bede was a Christian teacher first and an historian very much second.' How far is this a fair assessment?
3. 'Bede was a fine stylist, but had few other qualities of the true historian'. How far do you agree with this view?

You must also be prepared to answer broader questions, such as:

4. 'There were no true historians throughout the Middle Ages and the period of the Renaissance'.

When answering this question do not forget to offer a definition of 'true historian' (see page 3).

Source-based questions on 'Christian Historiography'

1. *Bede and his sources*
Read the extracts from Bede on page 33 and page 38. Answer the following questions, and continue to bear in mind the need to offer textual references to support your arguments.

a) What do Bede's comments on his sources suggest about his likely accuracy? (8 marks)
b) Comment on the range of sources used by Bede. (4 marks)

2. *Bede and his purpose*
a) What does Bede offer as the purpose of his *Ecclesiastical History*? (3 marks)
b) What effect might Bede's stated purpose have on his accuracy? (5 marks)

3 From The Enlightenment of the Eighteenth Century to Leopold von Ranke and the Rankean Tradition

1 The Enlightenment

To become enlightened, one must previously have been languishing and suffering in shadowy darkness. The eighteenth-century European intellectual movement known as the Enlightenment self-consciously demanded that one should recognise the defects of old attitudes and escape through embracing the new. The evils of the seventeenth-century wars of religion offered object lessons to the increasingly-wealthy intellectuals of the eighteenth century, whose ideas could flourish in a period of rapid, cheap printing and increasing literacy. For the first time, it seemed, men of ideas did not scruple to attack the Church - particularly the Catholic Church - for allegedly shackling the intellect of mankind, for attempting to hold back progress and for weaving webs of superstition which served to maintain the power of the clergy at the cost of the suffering and deaths of untold thousands in conflicts which should never have happened.

The 'man of sense' of the Enlightenment was therefore no friend to established religion. He appreciated the way in which the thinkers of his day interpreted the world in a critical, enquiring, rational but, above all, *secular* spirit. God's revelation was not an adequate explanation for the world as it was. In particular, he turned to the writings of the *philosophes* for instruction. The English translation 'philosophers' will hardly suffice: the German version *Aufklärer* or 'enlighteners' is better. From writers such as Voltaire or from the *Encyclopédie* edited by Diderot and d'Alembert, he would be encouraged to visualise a society based on an understanding of human nature and the laws governing human behaviour. He would learn that it was not enough to dream: that the man of sense was a propagandist and an activist whose aim must be to improve education, the legal system and administration and to encourage religious toleration and freedom of the intellect.

This is not to say that the *philosophes* spoke with one voice. For example, one of the most famous of them, Jean-Jacques Rousseau from Geneva, might write at one time for Diderot's *Encyclopédie*, but he did not share the assumption of many of his fellow contributors that science and intellectual freedom would lead to progress. Mankind, Rousseau felt, needed to be led into virtue: no society could be virtuous without an organised religious faith. But, despite his distance from other *philosophes*, there are key elements in common. Rousseau's approach rested upon his observation and experience, his refusal to argue by quoting dogmatic religion, his dissatisfaction with the old systems of government in the European monarchies - the *ancien régime* - and on his willingness to use his reason to evaluate systems of government and to point to a better future.

2 Enlightenment Historiography

It is hardly surprising that *philosophes* should write history. After all, history offered examples of behaviour which might be used to illustrate or support generalisations or laws about human nature. This is different in kind from the examples used by Renaissance historians, who, as we saw in Chapter 2, almost always brought a Christian world-view to bear on the moral and political lessons beloved of their classical masters. Most *philosophes* felt that the good man and the good Christian were mutually exclusive and made their attitude very clear. In this as in other things, they believed they had every right to be judgemental. Enlightenment historiography was also different in kind from the writings of many seventeenth and early eighteenth century historians who produced massively detailed factual works which were full to overflowing with references but weak in narrative thrust. Voltaire called them *érudits* (the 'learned ones') with more than a tinge of sarcasm. In his view, they were pursuing mouldy futilities in dark corners with stuttering candles: the philosophic historian would light up the entire room, even if that meant ignoring the nooks and crannies of mere detail. History could be used to identify the development of 'civilisation' - a term coined in the eighteenth century. This meant that history should be about the development of manners, customs, legal and political institutions, rather than an obsessive recounting of military and political matters. The tracing of that development rested upon the assumption that human nature and behaviour were constant through time, and therefore dependent on those identifiable generalisations referred to above.

One last point needs to be made about the *philosophes* and their writing of history. All were keen popularisers, in the sense that they wanted their works to be accessible to polite society throughout Europe. But they were not intended to be rallying cries for the masses, even though later enemies claimed that the writings of Rousseau and Voltaire led directly to the excesses of the French Revolution.

3 Edward Gibbon (1737-94)

Perhaps the greatest historian in the disparate group of *philosophes* was the Englishman Edward Gibbon. Some brief biographical points will help our assessment of Gibbon as an historian. A sickly child, Gibbon took the opportunity of a patchy formal education to read voraciously. Sent to Magdalen College, Oxford just before his sixteenth birthday, he was horrified by the lack of scholarship, greed and laziness of the tutors. His anger persisted into his unfinished memoirs, where he wrote:

> From the toil of reading or thinking or writing they had absolved their conscience, and the first shoots of learning and ingenuity withered on the ground ...

Short of murdering the entire college hierarchy, Gibbon came up with the best possible way of showing how much he despised Oxford, which was committed to maintaining the Anglican (Protestant) ascendancy: he converted to Catholicism. His horrified father dispatched him to the care of Daniel Pavilliard, a Protestant pastor in Lausanne, Switzerland. Pavilliard recognised the intellectual capacity of his charge and encouraged him to read the works of the *philosophes*. Sure enough, the five-year stay in Lausanne stripped Gibbon of his Catholicism, but it also stripped him of his Christianity. His French was now sufficiently fluent for his first published work to appear in that language: *Essai sur l'étude de la Littérature* (1761). He was to make the acquaintance of Diderot, d'Alembert and Voltaire. The first volume of his great work, *The History of the Decline and Fall of the Roman Empire*, was published in 1776: the final of six volumes appeared in 1788. After a period as a totally ineffectual MP in Britain, he decided to settle in Lausanne. The last year of his life was spent in England: he died in 1794.

4 Gibbon as a Philosophic Historian

The *Decline and Fall* owed a great deal to Voltaire and Montesquieu. Gibbon's opening paragraphs reflect the *philosophes'* concern with civilisation:

> ı In the second century of the Christian era, the empire of Rome comprehended the fairest part of the earth, and the most civilised portion of mankind. The frontiers of that extensive monarchy were guarded by ancient renown and disciplined valour. The gentle but
> 5 powerful influence of laws and manners had gradually cemented the union of the provinces.

Gibbon's stance on the early (and medieval) Christian Church was little different to that of Voltaire. He regarded Christianity of that time with considerable contempt. He treated Jesus himself with much respect, but theologians, priests and particularly monks or hermits (whose spirituality was world-denying) are presented as hypocritical, superstitious, wilfully obscure, fanatical, bigoted and nonsensical.

One can trace other similarities in the world-view of Gibbon and of the French *philosophes*. Assumptions he made about the decadence of the Orient and its allegedly corrupting effect on the Emperors are reminiscent of Montesquieu's comments on the effect of warm climates in *Spirit of the Laws*. His belief that great empires tend inevitably to their own dissolution is an echo of a number of writers, including Montesquieu (in his essay *Considerations on the Greatness and Decadence of the Romans* of 1734). In his *General Observations on the fall of the Roman Empire in the West*, Gibbon commented '... the decline of Rome was the natural and inevitable effect of immoderate greatness' (see page 52).

And so, the intellectual climate of the *philosophe* is very much the climate of Gibbon. But, when it came to the writing of a work of history, clear differences emerge. Here, Gibbon demonstrated his respect for the disciplined scholarship of the seventeenth century *érudits* through his frequent complaints about the failure of his fellow *philosophes* to respect the vital importance of factual evidence and the need to cite it as proof. In other words, he disliked the near-sociological system-building of many *philosophes* for the simple reason that it seemed to him to be fundamentally unhistorical in that it was not derived from fact. There was plenty of praise for Montesquieu, but he was also variously accused of 'strange', 'whimsical' and 'inexcusable' errors of interpretation and fact. Voltaire's errors were also relentlessly exposed. At one point, Gibbon commented:

> M. de Voltaire, unsupported by either fact or probability, has generously bestowed the Canary Islands on the Roman Empire.

There was, no doubt, the element of enjoyment here in ticking off one's peers, but I would argue that Gibbon was inclined to find factual errors inexcusable because it was, he believed, on fact that his own explanations were based. This is not to say that Gibbon felt that the correct writing of history was that of the *érudits*. Such antiquarianism - in the sense of an obsession with obscure data - was, on its own, as bad as unrestrained philosophic theorising.

In short, Gibbon saw the good historian as a combination of the *érudit* and the *philosophe*. In one footnote, he offered unstinting praise to just such a combination:

> See an excellent dissertation on the origin and migrations of nations, in the *Memoires de l'Académie des Inscriptions*, tom. xviii. p. 48-71. It is seldom that the antiquarian and the philosopher are so happily blended.

There are, in fact, over 8,000 footnotes in *Decline and Fall*. If Gibbon's referencing and love of detail is his inheritance from the *érudits*, his tone of complete self-confidence in his own judgements is his inheritance from the *philosophes*. So, too, is his tendency to assume that human nature is unchanging. However, there is a fundamental difference between Gibbon and other *philosophes* in the way in which inevitable gaps in the historical record were tackled. The majority of *philosophes*, rather than try to resolve them as far as possible by historical means, simply plastered over the whole issue with generalisations based on their supposed understanding of human behaviour. Gibbon did not ignore the gaps in this way. In acknowledging them, he also acknowledged that one should treat the past with sympathy rather than impatience. In his relationship with history, Gibbon had some of the patience of a lover. Most *philosophes* treated the past like a prostitute.

5 Gibbon and Causation

Gibbon's treatment of causation has been much criticised by modern historians. It has been argued that, not only was he biased against Christianity, but also that he failed to offer an in-depth analysis of causes of various types (political, economic, social, etc.) and a clear indication of their relative importance. On the other hand, of course, it could be claimed that, just because we expect this type of causal analysis nowadays, we have no right to demand it of Gibbon unless he set out to provide it. The short answer is that he did not. After all, his book is not titled *The Causes of the Decline and Fall of the Roman Empire.* Gibbon wrote a narrative history in which the characteristics of Roman civilisation were more worthy of attention than an account of causes. This is not to say that causes are completely ignored. In his *General Observations on the Fall of the Roman Empire in the West,* Gibbon offered a rather hasty summary:

1   The rise of a city, which swelled into an empire, may deserve, as a singular prodigy, the reflection of a philosophic mind. But the decline of Rome was the natural and inevitable effect of immoderate greatness ... The story of its ruin is simple and obvious; and instead of inquiring *why*
5   the Roman Empire was destroyed, we should rather be surprised that it had subsisted for so long ... [under the Emperors] the vigour of the military government was relaxed and finally dissolved by the partial institutions of Constantine; and the Roman world was overwhelmed by a deluge of barbarians ...
10   As the happiness of a future life is the great object of religion, we may hear without surprise or scandal that the introduction, or at least the abuse of Christianity, had some influence on the decline and fall of the Roman Empire ... The sacred indolence of the monks was devoutly embraced by a servile and effeminate age ... If the decline of the Roman
15   Empire was hastened by the conversion of Constantine, his victorious religion broke the violence of the fall, and mollified the ferocious temper of the conquerors.

This is indeed a fair summary of the points made in passing by Gibbon, although the balanced and rather cautious references to the link between Christianity and the fall of the Empire are a little surprising in their moderation. It is interesting to note that, when Gibbon discussed the writing of *Decline and Fall* in his *Memoirs,* the only cause of decline referred to is the growth of Christianity:

> ... I believed, and as I still believe, that the propagation of the gospel and triumph of the Church are inseparably connected with the decline of the Roman monarchy ...

6 Gibbon's Style

There are those historians, such as G.R. Elton, who would argue that the only sound reason for reading Gibbon nowadays is to enjoy his style. I do not agree, and intend to use this section to explore how Gibbon's frequently ironic style is not simply a bolt-on extra which is more attractive than the history beneath. Instead, we should see it as a reflection of the mind of an historian who had important things to say about the writing of history and who said much of it through his style.

Having said this, perhaps we should at least appreciate the way Gibbon's irony works. In the first place, we have the irony of understatement:

> 1 [Of Pope John XII] we read with some surprise ... that the Lateran palace was turned into a school for prostitution; and that his rapes of virgins and widows had deterred the female pilgrims from visiting the tomb of St Peter, lest, in the devout act, they should be violated by his
> 5 successor. The Protestants have dwelt with malicious pleasure on these characters of antichrist; but to a philosophic eye the vices of the clergy are far less dangerous than their virtues.

The reader is invited to consider an utterly appalling list of papal crimes, with Gibbon suggesting that it comes as 'some surprise' to us. Indeed! And then, in the same example, we enjoy an ironic reversal as Gibbon asks us to consider that such vices are less dangerous than clerical virtues. In the next example, the irony works through incongruity (i.e. misplacement), as Ladislaus performs his devotions in the midst of a list of barbaric savageries:

> Besieging Rome by land and water, he [Ladislaus, King of Naples] thrice entered the gates as a barbarian conqueror; profaned the altars, violated the virgins, pillaged the merchants, performed his devotions at St Peter's, and left a garrison in the castle of St Angelo.

There is also the irony of apparent approval or approbation. The truly gruesome self-castration performed by Origen is introduced from Origen's point of view as a sensible action. The irony is effective because it makes his behaviour seem even more unspeakably fanatical and ludicrous than any simple statement of Gibbon's opinion possibly could.

> ... the primitive church was filled with a great number of persons of either sex who had devoted themselves to the profession of perpetual chastity. A few of these, among whom we may reckon the learned Origen, judged it the most prudent to disarm the tempter.

The footnote reads:

> Before the fame of Origen had excited envy and persecution, this extra-ordinary action was rather admired than censured. As it was his general practice to allegorise Scripture, it seems unfortunate that, in this instance only, he should have adopted the literal sense.

All I have done so far, of course, is to suggest that Gibbon was very good at irony. But does his style - ironic or otherwise - serve any other purpose? I very much agree with Roy Porter that Gibbon is seeking first and foremost to engage his readers and to challenge them by putting himself before them with the invitation to consider the work-ings of his mind and his imagination as, together, they tackle histor-ical fact. In so doing, readers must use their own intellect and imagi-nation: through these means, history comes alive. It cannot do so through the antiquarian's obsessive failure to narrate; nor can it do so through the fundamentally unhistorical theorising of the *philosophe*.

In short, Gibbon does engage the reader, does appeal to his intelli-gence through the style and so does pull him into the story he tells - almost in the sense of a dramatist inviting the audience to share in his play. Let us remind ourselves of the opening paragraph of *Decline and Fall*.

1 In the second century of the Christian era, the empire of Rome comprehended the fairest part of the earth, and the most civilised portion of mankind. The frontiers of that extensive monarchy were guarded by ancient renown and disciplined valour. The gentle but
5 powerful influence of laws and manners had gradually cemented the union of the provinces. The peaceful inhabitants enjoyed and abused the advantages of wealth and luxury. The image of a free constitution was preserved with decent reverence: the Roman senate appeared to possess the sovereign authority, and devolved on the emperors all the
10 executive powers of government.

The introduction of the word 'abused' into the sentence 'The peaceful inhabitants enjoyed and abused the advantages of wealth and luxury' is something of a shock after the initially positive opening, and carries with it an interpretation that the reader must now note and await further development. In fact, Gibbon was fond of challenging the reader with two adjectives in close proximity which carry strikingly different meanings. The attentive reader then notices that Gibbon chooses the words 'image' and 'appeared' to make us question the apparent freedom of the constitution and power of the Senate. It would have been easier, perhaps, for Gibbon to have stated that the power of the Senate was much less than it appeared to be. But he is enticing the reader to accompany him and to allow two minds to work together.

This is not to suggest that Gibbon's irony or style as a whole is never self-indulgent, or that his many judgements are always the product of his desire to engage the reader in intellectual and imaginative gymnastics. No doubt there are times when he said things because they were clever, funny or both.

7 Gibbon's Purpose

We have noted Gibbon's sophistication, and therefore should not expect him to have written a history claiming to teach straightforward political or moral lessons. Some historians have argued that Gibbon was keen to use the *Decline and Fall* as an opportunity to reflect on the British Empire and its struggle with its American colonies between 1775 and 1783: the American War of Independence (or American Revolution, as it is termed in the USA). But beyond some rather teasing references to the revolt of the Armorican (echo of 'American', of course) provinces of the Roman Empire (northern France), no analogies were made. Naturally enough, as the whole work was shaped by Gibbon's personality and philosophic ideals, his opinions and arguments reflected eighteenth-century concerns. Gibbon's various comments on civic virtue and his preferences for a 'mixed constitution', where political power was not restricted to one man or one group, were no doubt interesting enough to MPs in a constitutional monarchy. But we recall that Gibbon aimed to enter into a dialogue with his readers: to challenge, to provoke, to engage and to encourage them to consider his views on the nature of civilisation and how it could and should progress through the curbing of priest-ridden superstition. All this would stimulate the intellect and arouse the imagination. He neither wanted nor expected readers to draw simplistic lessons as if history somehow repeated itself. It clearly did not.

8 Gibbon: a Conclusion

1 To the literary mind, the great English historians may be Clarendon, Gibbon and Macaulay, even though hardly anyone reads them any longer and their readability is their main claim to fame. Surely, they are worth reading and wrote splendid books, but they wrote in the prehis-
5 toric age ...[1]

So said the historian Geoffrey Elton, and his rather dismissive comments need to be considered carefully. By 'prehistoric age', Elton was referring to the periods before the professionalisation of history, when, stimulated by the work of Leopold von Ranke, history developed a methodology which rested upon the principles of objectivity and 'scientific' source evaluation (see pages 59-62). By these criteria, Gibbon is clearly found wanting. Although he stressed the virtues of impartiality, Gibbon did not claim that the historian could or should distance himself from his writing. One should have respect for the facts - hence the need for impartiality - but history was given shape by the dialogue between historian and reader. In terms of source evaluation, Gibbon is indeed open to criticism. He fully accepted the Enlightenment spirit of rational inquiry and questioned his sources shrewdly and critically but without a systematic technique. He had no firm and consistent method for assessing reliability, and failed to allow for the way in which the nature of the source related to the author's purpose and so affected its value. And, as Momigliano puts it, Gibbon 'never went beyond a superficial impression of the comparative value of his sources.'[2] On the other hand, he was adept at identifying bias and in sifting a source to exploit its value and discard its irrelevancies.

No-one would deny that Gibbon used a considerable quantity of sources, but did he use a full range? He was not entirely restricted to literary sources, as he was interested in and made some use of inscriptions, medals, coins and architecture. But he relied on published sources - in the main, the contents of his own, well-stocked library. He never mastered palaeography (the study of ancient handwriting) or diplomatic (the analysis of the forms of documents) and so could not make use of original documents. Nor did his understanding of German allow him to exploit the relevant researches of German scholars.

Gibbon, like other philosophic historians, is open to the criticism that his willingness to judge rested on an assumption that human motivation followed from patterns of behaviour which remained constant through time. He, like them, did not consider that each age should be judged on its own terms, rather than have standards from another time imposed upon it. The perspective that each age was unique was a characteristic of Ranke's history (see pages 59-60).

On one level, then, Elton's criticisms seem well-founded. But there are major objections to be made to them. First, we should never forget to praise Gibbon for the extraordinary range, erudition (scholarship) and fundamental accuracy of his monumental work. After all, he covered the history of the Empire both east and west (based in Rome and Byzantium/Constantinople) from the second century AD through to the fall of Constantinople in the fifteenth century. He discussed the rise, not only of Christianity, but also of Islam and was interested in the Persian Empire as well. Burrow reminds us that a work on this scale which supersedes Gibbon has yet to be written.[3] And, when one assesses Gibbon's scholarship by the Rankean standards, then his factual accuracy is nothing less than astonishing. Secondly, as we shall see in Chapter 5, we cannot afford to accept without question (as Elton appears to do) that correct, objective history is attainable and can be communicated without using literary techniques which would cloud objectivity. In a way, Gibbon's habit of directly addressing the reader and inviting him to enter into the mind of the historian is more up-to-date than the denial that this should or does happen. Of course, writing a work like *Decline and Fall* which is so clearly individualistic, idiosyncratic and personal means that one is unlikely to encourage imitators. Gibbon therefore founded no school of historians. But he has nonetheless left an invaluable legacy. He pioneered the secular treatment of religious history. He reminds us that, in the end, history must engage the reader. Gibbon's irony pulls us into his writing, makes us want to understand, invites us to use our intellect and leaves us with the feeling that human nature is itself ironical in its complexity. The excellent book by John Clive, *Not by Fact Alone*,[4] reminds us that Gibbon and other great historians were able to make the reader feel a sense of personal involvement in the events being described and that amusement and instruction complemented each other very well.

9 Leopold von Ranke (1795-1886) and the Professionalisation of History

Ranke is a favourite with students answering examination questions on the methodology and nature of history. It is easy to understand why. On the face of it, Ranke had a near-revolutionary impact on historiography. The standard answer to a question on the contribution of Ranke to historiography runs something like this.

> 1 Reacting against the system-building and generalisations of the Enlightenment, he claimed that one should study the past for its own sake and respect the uniqueness of each age. In the search for history 'as it actually happened', he not only came up with a new historical
> 5 technique based on rigid objectivity but also single-handedly created the history profession - complete with professors of repute, seminars, and a stress on original documentary research as the mark of the real historian.

The student who remembers to evaluate as well as to describe often points out that Ranke has been criticised for over-stating the possibility of objectivity, and that his own objectivity can be called into question, since he wrote from a conservative, pro-Prussian viewpoint. It might also be pointed out that Ranke focused purely on the history of the élites and on diplomatic and political history, and so, although his emphasis on rigorous scholarship remains to this day, history has expanded into a much fuller and broader concern with the totality of human experience.

There is certainly caricature - or over-simplification - in the sample answer above, but then caricature can hardly work without some element of truth. The task will be to assess how much. But there is an additional complication in that, although it is important to try to establish what Ranke actually represented and what his ideas were, it is also important to establish what those he influenced *thought* his ideas were. As we shall see, there were those who claimed inspiration from Ranke for positions he would not have recognised as his own.

10 Ranke's Background and Enlightenment Historiography

Ranke was born in the small town of Wiehe in Thuringia, Germany. In the late eighteenth century, Germany was not a nation-state but was a loose grouping - alliance is far too strong a term - of over 300 separate states which owed allegiance on paper to the Holy Roman Emperor (in practice, a member of the Habsburg family, with a power-base in Austria). The greatest potential challenge to Habsburg predominance (such as it was) within Germany came from the Kings of Prussia (the Hohenzollern dynasty). More to the point, German nationalism, fanned by the experience of, and opposition to, the expansion of France in the revolutionary and Napoleonic eras (1789-1815), was increasingly significant as the nineteenth century progressed. There were several possible routes to a German nation-state, but one which earned the support of most of those who preferred time-honoured systems of government was through the expansion of the kingdom of Prussia. In the event, it was through this route that the German Empire was established by 1871. Ranke's birthplace had been part of the independent kingdom of Saxony, but the area was annexed by Prussia in 1815. Iggers and Moltke[5] rightly point out that Ranke was therefore by no means emotionally committed to Prussia itself, and that the image of a more federal Germany (i.e. made up of states which retained some independence) was an appealing one for him.

Of even greater importance in the making of Ranke the historian were his deeply-felt Lutheran religious beliefs. Ranke entered the University of Leipzig in 1814 to study Theology and Philology (the science of language). Significantly, he never completed his theological studies because he objected to the university faculty's cool, rationalistic approach to faith. Ranke's God was not to be pigeon-holed or labelled in any such atmosphere of calm deduction; His presence was reflected in past and present events, but, because of the distance between God and humanity, one should not presume to reveal or uncover Him fully or simplistically. But God was not separate from history. This religious belief linked with strands in German Idealist philosophy - particularly the work of Fichte - which Ranke found appealing (or so his early notes and correspondence suggest). He sympathised with Fichte's concept of the role of the true scholar in uncovering something of the 'divine idea' from the world as we perceive it.

Clearly there were aspects of Enlightenment thought which were unlikely to impress Ranke. He detested Voltaire's attacks on organised religion, and rational systematising would fit uneasily with his concept of the relationship between what the human mind could do and its limits in uncovering the ultimate truth which was God. On the other hand, since God lay behind the unfolding of human history, there ought to be some sort of meaning or discernible purpose therein, even though it would be wrong and presumptuous to identify a precise pattern. With this in mind, Ranke was attracted to the thought of the philosopher Herder. Herder argued that there was not some sort of Enlightenment-style widespread progress in rationality throughout history, but a God-given flowering of separate national cultures. His contention was that one must seek to understand a period on its own terms and by studying its own unique set of values: an approach which has sometimes been labelled 'historicism'. Historicism is not my favourite term - largely because it has been applied to approaches to history which are markedly dissimilar. But, since it is often used in connection with Ranke, we ought at least to recognise that he can be called historicist in the sense of rejecting both the secular-spirited system-building of the *philosophes* and the way in which they ignored what was unique to each age. Ranke was also inclined to blame the *philosophes* for providing the intellectual fuel for what he saw as the mindless, irreligious and destructive machine that was the French Revolution.

It would therefore seem that my sample answer was accurate in suggesting that Ranke rejected all that the Enlightenment stood for. This is basically true, but it should also be said that some *Aufklärer* of Germany were at odds with French *philosophes* in retaining a strong religious conviction. This in turn led the *Aufklärer* to deny that natural laws could 'explain' the insights of spirituality. And so, it would be safer to argue that Ranke rejected the arguments of the Enlightenment as propounded by the French *philosophes*. This will at least prevent us from assuming that the Enlightenment was an entirely unified movement.

11 Ranke and *'wie es eigentlich gewesen'*

Ranke's first published work was *Histories of the Latin and Germanic Nations* (1824), written when he was a schoolteacher of History and Classics. In his preface, Ranke wrote:

> To history has been given the function of judging the past, of instructing men for the profit of future years. The present attempt does not aspire to such a lofty undertaking. It merely wants to show how, essentially, things happened.

How, essentially, things happened: 'wie es eigentlich gewesen'. Nowadays, this phrase is usually translated 'how things really (or actually) happened'. Iggers[6] points out that, in the nineteenth century, the term 'eigentlich' meant, not only 'actually', but also 'essentially' or 'characteristically'. Iggers believes that Ranke's meaning was closer to 'essentially' than 'actually', and that his famous phrase is not the endorsement of history as the recovery of facts that historians then and since have believed it to be. Given Ranke's religious views and his belief that God's presence in history could be glimpsed - perhaps the essence of history - this argument is indeed plausible. However, there are occasions when Ranke's commitment to uncovering facts is stated with less ambiguity:

> Strict presentation of facts, no matter how conditional and unattractive they might be, is undoubtedly the supreme law.

There is certainly no doubt that Ranke expressed a clear distaste for judging the past or trying to make use of it for present ends - such as teaching political lessons. The past is to be studied on its own terms, with appropriate recognition of the value-systems unique to each age. His preface to the *Histories of the Latin and Germanic Nations* (quoted below) concludes in ringing phrases which remind us of the essential - or actual - difficulty in understanding Ranke on his own terms. He is inviting us to put aside our present values, to avoid judging, to attempt to recreate the events of the past. And yet he adds that, at some point, we should be able to detect (however unclearly) the intentions of God. One is tempted to suggest that doing so may in practice mean imposing a value-system on the past. Ranke is demanding an objectivity from the historian, but at the same time suggesting what that objectivity should lead to. This is, perhaps, an awkward approach. On the other hand, one should see it as a two-stage process in which the first stage is more certain than the second. The historian starts with his objective analysis to uncover facts about the past. Having done so, and without imposing any theory of his own, he should then be able to move from the particular to the general. In this second stage, his generalisations may hint at the vaguest of outlines of God's intentions. In contemplating such possibilities, Ranke's prose takes on a religious tone:

> I A lofty ideal does exist: to grasp the event itself in its human comprehensiveness, its unity, and its fullness. It should be possible to attain this goal. I know how far I am from having achieved it. One tries, one strives, but in the end one has not reached the goal. Only let no one become
> 5 impatient about this failure ... our subject is mankind as it is, explicable or inexplicable, the life of the individual, of the generations, of the peoples, and at times the hand of God over them.

How, then, does one go about recovering the past as it was? Fundamental here is the critical technique used by Ranke, although it has to be said that he never wrote a treatise on method as such. I have already suggested that objectivity was the appropriate Rankean frame of mind. Writing about his *English History, Principally in the Seventeenth Century* (1859), he said that he had tried to 'extinguish my own self, as it were, to let the things speak ...' In other words, he claimed to let the past speak for itself. It is vital to appreciate that, to Ranke, the past spoke through original documentary sources. In the memorable phrase of Lord Acton, Regius Professor of Modern History at Cambridge at the end of the nineteenth century, Ranke was the 'real originator of the heroic study of records.'

However, Ranke was looking for more than straightforward factual information about dates or events from his sources. The feelings or ideas of those who produced the sources were as meaningful and true - or more meaningful and more true - than, say, verifiable events.

So, although Ranke left no manual on 'how to do history', his stress on objectivity, his demand for archival research and a willingness to use such sources to provide information on attitudes and feelings must be seen as highly influential. On the strength of his first published book, Ranke was appointed to the University of Berlin and swiftly instituted a seminar system of instruction which enabled him to pass on his critical methods, and so to shape the coming generation of scholars.

We should, perhaps, at this point consider both how effectively Ranke maintained his objectivity and also how well his techniques of source analysis worked. Of course, Ranke could be criticised in that he wrote about issues of interest to him: perhaps the totally objective historian would have deliberately chosen those of no personal interest. But surely to complain because he understandably wanted to write about peoples, nations and the interface between politics and religion would be unfair. It would be another matter if his discussion of nations led to him upholding Prussia or Germany as a whole as somehow 'the best' or most deserving. This does not happen. As we have seen, Ranke is keen to explore links between different peoples, and was no slavish supporter of Prussian control of a new Germany: his preferences, we recall, appear to have been in the direction of a more federal Germany. Another good testing ground of his objectivity should be his *History of the Popes* (1834). As a Lutheran and a German, he might be expected to take every opportunity to attack the Roman Catholic Church. In fact, Ranke emerges from the test rather well. For example, his criticisms of the Church at the time of the Reformation are generally more calm and considered than angry and unfair. In commenting on the Pope who excommunicated Luther, he said:

> ... in the court of Leo X there were few things deserving blame in themselves, although we cannot but perceive that his pursuits might have been more strictly in accordance with his position as supreme head of the Church.

On the other hand, in the 1871 edition of his papal history, Ranke tackled the recent defeat of Catholic France by Prussia. He clearly found it difficult to preserve his objectivity, and so sheltered (not very successfully) behind what a 'convinced Protestant' might think:

I A state [Prussia] prevailed which had risen in antagonism to the exclusive rule of the papacy, and which now had also became the champion of the German cause. It attained a position which guaranteed an impor-

tant part in the universal political and religious movements of the world.
5 A convinced Protestant would say this was the divine decision against
   the pretensions of the Pope who claimed that he was the sole inter-
   preter of the faith and of the divine mysteries on earth.

Despite the occasional lapse of this type, Iggers concludes that 'Ranke
achieves a remarkable degree of impartiality'.[7] His technique of
scrupulously allowing the facts to emerge from the sources before
considering the general issues must have contributed to this success.

In analysing Ranke's technique of source evaluation, I want to make
use of an assessment by Gino Benzoni[8] of Ranke's work on what was
undoubtedly his favourite source: the Venetian *Relazioni*, or reports
made by the Venetian ambassadors to various countries and to the
papal court after the completion of their missions. Benzoni describes
Ranke's excitement in discovering the potential of these sources,
offering as they did a superb insight by intelligent eyewitnesses into
the great events of the time (and also into the characteristics of the
states with which they were familiar). So Ranke's enthusiasm is understandable, and also reflects his view that first-hand information was
inevitably better than contemporary or subsequent narratives (or
literary evidence, for that matter). But herein lies Ranke's problem,
because the *Relazioni* were treated by him far too incautiously. He
neglected to consider how far they were distorted by the style of the
day or the understandable desire of the ambassadors to impress their
superiors. They were also distorted by the ambassadors' inevitable
assumptions of prior knowledge amongst the recipients and by their
upper-class outlook.

Ranke was making every effort to free original sources from their
past neglect, but, as we have seen, there was a sense in which he
became their prisoner. As with the *Relazioni*, he was so excited by what
they had to offer that his critical technique failed to exploit them.
Also, as a pioneer in the field of archival research, he was not always
able to gain access to collections which would have made his research
far more valuable. The Vatican archives were closed to him, and the
Venetian authorities were often obstructive. Such limitations mean
that Ranke's work itself has long been superseded.

12 Ranke's Subject-Matter and Style

One might, perhaps, expect that Ranke's books would be detailed
and narrow in range: fathers of the earnest modern PhD thesis,
perhaps. This would seem to follow from his insistence on thorough
research and evaluation. In fact, we get sweeping narrative histories
written - and this again is a surprise - with considerable flair for
making the most of dramatic possibilities. How can we account for
Ranke's subject-matter and style?

Firstly, we should recall Ranke's interest in some aspects of the thought of Herder and Fichte. The latter's view that a love for the life of the past could lead to God clearly complements Ranke's view that the proper study of history was a contribution to knowing what we could of God. Herder, the philosopher of nationality, offered the spirit of the Volk - an almost untranslatable word, with meanings including a people, a sense of nationhood and shared culture - as the motive force of history, because within the Volk is the divine spirit. Herder was adamant that Völker (in the plural) arising through history were to be studied on their own terms and without any attempt to judge. It is significant that so much of Ranke's work should focus on the history of peoples, and that he should speak of nations being 'ideas of the divine spirit'. Here we see again the spirituality which appears to lead to Ranke identifying God's will in history - to trace patterns, in fact. But, once again, Ranke will not fall into what he sees as the trap: to system-atise, to force history into a particular mould, to have the arrogance to claim to know God's purposes, for that would mean knowing God - the ultimate presumption. In the 1830s, Ranke jotted down comments on the relationship between history and philosophy. He wrote:

1   Two qualities are necessary to form a true historian. The first is a feeling for and a joy in the particular in and by itself. He will try to comprehend all ... without any purpose other than joy in the individual life ... without thinking how the whole appears in the particular. This, however,
5   is not all. It is necessary that the historian keep his eyes open for the general. He will not have preconceived ideas as does the philosopher, but rather while observes the particular, the course which the develop-ment of the world in general has taken will be revealed to him.

This would seem to be a difficult balancing act. On the one hand, the historian must objectively, and without a head full of theories, allow the sources to speak to him: the joy of the particular. On the other hand, there comes a point in the course of this study of the particular that significant connections are somehow made. Ranke saw in this the hand of God, leading peoples into power on the world stage: for, he says, 'no state has ever existed without a spiritual basis and a spiritual content. In power itself a spiritual essence manifests itself.' And so, Ranke wrote the histories of peoples who were significant in world history (by which he means European history): hence *Histories of the Latin and German Peoples, Princes and Peoples of Southern Europe: The Ottomans and the Spanish Monarchy, German History, 1555-1618* and *German History in the Age of the Reformation.* The *History of the Popes* fits the pattern because the power of the Roman Catholic Church made it a great player on the European/world stage. Now, an historian who sees in the history of the peoples a spiritual dimension will hanker after writing a world history: and it is no coincidence that, near the end of his long life, he should write his *Universal History* (1880). In his preface, Ranke said:

1   … it was impossible to remain content with the history of individual
     nations. A collection of national histories, whether on a larger or a
     smaller scale, is not what we mean by Universal History, for in such a
     work the general connection of things is liable to be obscured. To recog-
5   nise this connection, to trace the sequence of those great events which
     link all nations together and control their destinies, is a task which the
     science of Universal History undertakes.

Bearing in mind his interest in the relationships between nations and
the spirit of God lying behind them, one might expect Ranke to write
cultural history. He did not do so. Given the breadth of his themes -
and particularly the stress he placed on the relationship between
Church and State - it is perhaps inevitable that Ranke should have
concentrated on political history throughout his work. Specifically,
much of what he wrote focused on the monarchs and statesmen as
they dealt with international affairs. His desire to recognise the
connections between great events meant that he had to make a judg-
ment on which were most significant and which could be left out. In
his *Civil Wars and Monarchy in France in the Sixteenth and Seventeenth
Century*, he commented:

> I have not devoted much space to less significant events; but this has
> enabled me to pay the greater attention to those of world-historical
> importance.

But what did Ranke see as a significant event? In part, the significant
was that which was provided by the sources to which he had access -
diplomats' reports, letters, diaries: in other words, mainly records of
the élites about the élites. These were almost always couched in
personal terms, and so implicitly stressed the impact of the individual
on history. And, of course, he felt that significance lay in certain
events which captured the spirit or the moral energy of a nation and
which helped it to grow.

The style of Ranke is indeed something of a surprise. One might
reasonably expect to see the father of scientific history avoiding as far
as possible all literary devices in his narrative. In fact, as Peter Gay
argues, Ranke

> displayed the gifts we normally associate with storytellers or play-
> wrights: speed, colour, variety, freshness of diction, and superb control
> … he establishes his characters with the precision of a novelist.[9]

Perhaps we could argue that Ranke's stylistic devices and taste for
anecdotes reflect a recognition that to see the past as it actually was
is more than a merely intellectual exercise. It is an emotional and
spiritual one as well. In the *History of France*, Ranke argued that the
historian's task was both a science and an art. It had to match the
scientific demands of philology, whilst offering the reader the
appeal of imaginative literature.

13 Ranke's Contribution to Historiography

a) Introduction

I have suggested that Ranke's writing of history is more complex than our original picture of him as the would-be scientific/impartial prober of archives and historical technician. However, it is clear that Ranke's fellow historians frequently misunderstood and simplified his position. This is not to deny that Ranke's influence was profound. Historians in Europe and North America, hungry for academic respectability, seized on those aspects of his thought which appeared to give history a 'scientific' status: namely, the demand for research into original documents and the need for objectivity. In this way, Ranke did much to elevate the status of history as a discipline at university level. Many a history professor owed his new chair to the sudden professionalisation of the subject.

Of course, this meant that less clear or more inconvenient aspects were missed, distorted, ignored or criticised. German historians of the so-called Prussian school disliked Ranke's lack of enthusiasm for the unification of Germany through Prussian expansion, but they respected much of his methodology. Others - the so-called Neo-Rankeans - tried to adapt (i.e. distort) his ideas on relations between nations to justify the expansion of Imperial Germany at the end of the nineteenth century. But they too respected his methodology.

The impact of Ranke on British historiography similarly reflects a mixture of admiration for his method and an adapting or distorting of his achievement to suit personal agenda and/or political circumstances. The response of the Catholic intellectual Lord Acton (1834-1902), for example, is instructive. He recognised Ranke as his master and claimed that the latter

> 1 is the representative of the age which instituted the modern study of History. He taught it to be critical, to be colourless, and to be new. We meet him at every step, and he has done more for us than any other man … He decided effectually to repress the poet, the patriot, the reli-
> 5 gious or political partisan, to sustain no cause, to banish himself from his books…

Colourless? Unpoetic? To banish himself from his books? Surely Acton is wrong - and yet we can learn from his misinterpretations by suggesting that he saw in Ranke what he wanted to see, and in Ranke something of the history he wanted to write himself. What Ranke was able to offer Acton and others like him was a 'scientific' method that did not involve the kind of theorising which explained the past through laws of human behaviour which excluded God.

Similarly, those who objected to history being used to back up contemporary political attitudes - 'present-minded' history - had the tradition of Rankean-style historicism for support. A good example would be the British historian Herbert Butterfield; a Christian whose highly-influential book *The Whig Interpretation of History* (1931) attacked those who wrote history through the distorting glass of their political views. I want to look at Butterfield's views in some detail for three reasons. First of all, they allow us to explore that very significant tradition in British historiography which he was attacking and an historian, Thomas Babington Macaulay, who encapsulated that tradition. Secondly, Butterfield's criticisms themselves reflect a tradition developing in British post-Great War historiography which remains influential to this day. Thirdly, his warnings on the need to avoid 'present-mindedness' reflect themes discussed in Chapter 5 and the conclusion.

b) Herbert Butterfield, Whig History, and Present-Mindedness

Butterfield criticised those he labelled Whig historians on the grounds that they made assumptions about the direction history had taken: namely, towards a political system (British parliamentary democracy) of which they fully approved. Whig history was therefore nationalistic, liberal, optimistic, judgemental and teleological (written with a goal or ideal in mind).

Butterfield's *The Whig Interpretation of History* is an odd book. In the first place, it is surprisingly limited in scope. Astonishingly few historical themes are brought in to elucidate arguments: Luther and the Reformation appear with a regularity which becomes truly irritating. And few historians are mentioned by name; only one - Lord Acton - is discussed in any detail. In Lord Acton, it seems, the Whig historian 'reached his highest consciousness.' This might come as something of a surprise, given Acton's extremely positive attitude towards Rankean 'scientific' objectivity. But, to Butterfield, Acton was the essential Whig, not only because he made liberal moral judgements in his work, but also because he made morality the judge of good and bad historical writing. More obvious targets, perhaps, were historians like Thomas Babington Macaulay (1800-59) and his great-nephew George Macaulay Trevelyan (1876-1962), whose work did indeed trace the development of liberty in a suitably whiggish manner. Macaulay, for instance, started his monumental *The History of England* (four volumes, published 1855-61) with a hymn of praise to progress:

I ... unless I greatly deceive myself, the general effect of this chequered narrative will be to excite thankfulness in all religious minds, and hope in the breasts of all patriots. For the history of our country during the last hundred and sixty years is eminently the history of physical, of
5 moral, and of intellectual improvement.

He traced the origins of the English nation in the signing of the Magna Carta, which he saw as limiting the tyrannical power of the foreign, Norman kings. Further limits were placed on kingly despotism by the developing powers of parliament, and alongside these powers came prosperity. Liberty and prosperity both benefited from the individualism encouraged by Luther and the Protestant Reformation. In the time of Charles I an attempt was made to sabotage such progress. After the execution of the King, extremism flourished under the mercifully-brief Cromwellian republic before the Stuarts had a second chance to show that they could respect the constitution of England with the coronation of Charles II in 1660. Under his brother James II, a backward-looking Catholicism inevitably combined with a renewed despotism which was smashed by the Glorious Revolution of 1688, where the Whigs called upon William of Orange (as King William III) to rescue the traditional liberties of England.

This kind of whiggish history was an easy enough target. It was, of course, deeply anachronistic. Macaulay was fond of referring to the English of the past as 'we', so assuming that their thought-processes were earlier versions of those of the nineteenth-century liberal gentleman. He doled out praise to those on the side of progress and blame to those on the side of reaction. Setting out to persuade, he employed the most effective literary devices to convince the reader. Having decided (quite wrongly) that the Quaker William Penn was a reactionary hypocrite and traitor to William III, he made full use of emotive language and sarcasm (and untrustworthy sources) to blacken his name:

1   After about three years of wandering and lurking he [Penn], by the mediation of some eminent men ... made his peace with the government [of William III], and again ventured to resume his ministrations. The return which he made for the lenity with which he had been
5   treated does not much raise his character. Scarcely had he begun to harangue in public about the unlawfulness of war, when he sent a message earnestly exhorting James to make an immediate descent on England with thirty thousand men.

Macaulay very much enjoyed using the type of ironic contrast we see in the last sentence of his remarks on Penn. He also enjoyed the use of caricature. His portrait of Titus Oates, an admittedly sinister figure who falsely claimed to have uncovered a Popish Plot to murder Charles II, takes caricature to the outer limits. Oates is a villain in the manner of some classical and humanist historians.

> his short neck, his legs uneven ... as those of a badger, his forehead low as that of a baboon, his purple cheeks, and his monstrous length of chin ... those hideous features on which villainy seemed to be written by the hand of God.

In short, Macaulay's *History of England* made deliberate use of the techniques of imaginative literature because its author believed that the link between history and literature was an intimate one. In an early essay (1828) for the Whig periodical the *Edinburgh Review,* he argued that the perfect historian must strive to authenticate all facts, but that truth must be given 'those attractions which have been usurped by fiction.' It is, as we have seen, unlikely that a strict attachment to fact is likely to survive this kind of attachment to the techniques of fiction. Macaulay used direct speech for its vividness, but did not restrict himself to what he could claim as authentic from the written record. I very much like Owen Dudley Edward's comment (which also suggests the distance between Ranke and Macaulay):

> The idea of making the past speak for itself became the practice of making it speak through him.[10]

Allied to this was Macaulay's oft-quoted remark on his hope that his *History of England* would 'for a few days supersede the last fashionable novel on the tables of young ladies.' Macaulay was, of course, being a little disingenuous. His ambition was to write not only a genuinely popular work, but also one which would stand the test of time and be genuinely instructive. His readers were to appreciate the glories of the English brand of freedom and to accept that there was progress still to come as the parliamentary franchise was extended in the nineteenth century. But that progress should not be rushed. Did not his *History* warn of the dangers of extremism?

Butterfield's objections to this form of historical writing were not limited to its 'present-mindedness' and other distortions. He was obsessed with the evils of what he calls 'abridged' history, commenting 'indeed all history must tend to become more whig as it becomes more abridged.' This, it seems, comes about the further one removes oneself from the painstaking work of the research student. In fact, he argued that the danger of studying the past for the sake of the present 'is one that is really introduced for the purpose of facilitating the abridgement of history.' A typical abridgement, of course, is the wide-ranging, narrative, explanatory and popularised 'general history' in the manner of Macaulay. Small wonder that historians have seen Butterfield as one of the chief inspirations behind the post-war tendency for British historians to dislike the broader canvas and prefer the detailed study. J.H. Plumb, himself a believer in the importance of making history accessible to a wide audience, commented in 1969 that he felt the need to toll the bell for the passing of the great narrative histories, and that Butterfield's work opened the 'first fusillade'[11] of 'technical history' against them. Similar points are made by R.H.C. Davies, who comments:

> Butterfield himself had never intended that his work should cause historians to stop trying to explain history. But because he had demonstrated that the Whig historians had read their own ideas into historical events, lesser historians have felt timid of expressing any ideas at all.[12]

And yet, it would be a mistake to see in Butterfield nothing more than an advocate of the narrow scholarly monograph, written by the painstaking efforts of an historian who deliberately distanced himself from all the concerns of his own times. In *The Englishman and His History* (1944), Butterfield responded to the demands of the Second World War by accepting that the Whig version of history at least offered a shared set of values and a belief in liberty which had helped to unite the nation in opposition to Nazism. And, like Ranke, his deep Christian beliefs informed his whole conception of what history was and what historiography should be. In his view, Christianity, based on the historical Jesus, had the most intimate of relationships with history. Like Ranke, he would not presume to identify what God's intentions were, but was adamant that God did work in history and that, in the links between events, some awareness of his work was possible. To deny that God was at work within the world was, at the very best, to make him an absentee God. In *God in History* (1958), Butterfield complained that belief in an absentee God led to an optimism about the workings of the universe which made a personal religion unnecessary:

> And if God cannot play a part in life, that is to say, in history, then neither can human beings have very much concern about him or very real relationships with him.

One can, perhaps, link this with Butterfield's exasperation at the complacency of Whig history. Indeed, he had a very strong sense of the essential sinfulness of human nature which made optimism and a rather unthinking belief in progress doubly difficult to accept. Sin - and God's judgement on sin - fatally compromised all human system-building and institutions. In *Christianity and History* (1949), he complained of those who saw merely human political structures and organisations as being 'the actual end of life, the ultimate purpose of history' and proclaimed:

> 1 Though the judgment is always upon us - upon man's universal sin - the sentence falls on great human systems, on nations, civilisations, institutions; indeed on all the schematised patterns into which human life ranges itself in various periods... The very things which provide the neat
> 5 developing patterns in our history books - provide the supra-personal edifices like state, culture, capitalism, liberalism - and which are associated with the idea of progress, are the things which are shattered when the judgment falls on men.

To Butterfield, therefore, as for Ranke, it was vital for historians to study the past on its own terms without distorting it through their own present-day concerns and imposing on it their own pet models and theories. For those without religious beliefs, this was sufficient providing they did not attempt to find a meaning for life itself:

> Those who complain that technical history does not provide people with the meaning of life are asking from an academic science more than it can give …

For the Christian, the task was to engage in objective research and to make the past intelligible to the present day:

> having in his religion the key to his conception of the whole human drama, he can safely embark on a detailed study of mundane events, if only to learn through their inter-connections the ways of Providence.

It is clear that Butterfield's attitude towards historical writing was largely informed by his Christian beliefs, but it would be ill-advised to ignore the influence of the political upheavals through which he lived. The shock of the First World War and the economic crises of the Depression made a simplistic belief in progress hard to uphold. The Second World War, the Holocaust, the dangers of atomic warfare and the growing tensions of the Cold War had a similar effect. *Christianity and History* is full of references to the challenge of Marxism. Ranke saw the irreligious systematising of the Enlightenment as a threat to Christianity: Butterfield saw the irreligious systematising of Marxism in the same terms.

There is clearly something problematic in Butterfield's concept of what made good historical writing. In particular, we see a tension between his dismissal of 'present-minded' history and the fact that his vision of history was itself shaped by his own times. It was, in fact, the product of his own religious beliefs and the sense of crisis within his own society. Claims that historical writing should in essence be time-less (even if made meaningful to the present day) do not fit well with such a recognition. In any case, some of Butterfield's comments betray an inconsistency. He could even sound like Macaulay at times.

> 1 As far as I am concerned, the point of teaching history to undergradu-
> ates is to turn them into public servants and statesmen, in which case
> they had better believe in ideals, and not shrink from having ideas and
> policies and from carrying their policies through … I know it sounds
> 5 priggish - but I happen to think history is a school of wisdom and states-
> manship.

Not so much priggish, perhaps, as whiggish. It is, however, important to take into account the context of Butterfield's words. He was keen to distance himself from the highly-influential work of his contempo-rary Lewis Bernstein Namier (1888-1960) on the grounds that Namier was inclined to dismiss the impact of ideas on human conduct (a standpoint difficult for a Christian of the Butterfield mould to stomach). Nevertheless, there were clear links between Butterfield and Namier. A discussion of these links and the work of Namier himself will help to illuminate further the responses of histo-rians within the English historical tradition to the example of - and issues associated with - Rankean historiography.

c) Lewis Bernstein Namier

Sir Lewis Namier's immense influence on the British historical profession of the 1950s and 60s stemmed from the way in which his approaches appeared to coincide with the methodological, social and political stances prevalent within that profession. His painstaking scholarship and intensive archival research appealed to historians who increasingly accepted that such apparent Rankeanism was the basis of true historical writing. His work ran virtually parallel with that of Butterfield, and can also be seen as an attack on the confident, sweeping narratives of the Whigs. His distaste for theories (Whig or Marxist) which imposed patterns of progress on the past suited the conservative-minded historian shaken by the collapse of liberal optimism and the threat of Communism. In the years after the Second World War, Namier's élitism and obsession with the landed aristocracy offered an appealing alternative to those who disliked the increasing egalitarianism of Labour-led Britain.

Namier's main contribution to the development of British historiography was to avoid the standard narrative of the actions of an institution like the British parliament. Instead, his 'structural analysis', as it came to be called, uncovered its actual workings through his use of prosopography (collective biography). Avoiding the whiggish assumption that the ideals and policies of Whig and Tory parties shaped political behaviour, his researches into the backgrounds and aims of eighteenth-century MPs led him to argue that their main motivations were essentially personal. Political behaviour, then, was the result of self-interest, ambition and local rivalries rather than adherence to principle. In *The Structure of Politics at the Accession of George III* (1929) and *England in the Age of the American Revolution* (1930) he demolished other Whig convictions. George III was generally seen as the enemy of democratic progress and a king whose autocratic ways led directly to the loss of the American colonies in the American War of Independence (or American Revolution) of 1775-83. Namier attempted with some, albeit partial, success to rehabilitate the king by examining his personal papers and so arguing that there was no evidence of a desire to increase his own power at the expense of parliament. His opening chapter of *England in the Age of the American Revolution* (Macmillan, 1930) made the case:

1 ... George III never left the safe ground of Parliamentary government, and merely acted as *primus inter pares* [first among equals], the first among the borough-mongering, electioneering gentlemen of England. While the Stuarts tried to browbeat the House and circumscribe the
5 range of its action, George III fully accepted its constitution and recognised its powers ...

In Namier's view, the so-called Whig politicians were not to be seen as the defenders of British liberties against a Stuart-like would-be tyrant, but as selfish politicians who played the 'Constitution in danger!' card as a useful weapon in factional intrigue. And, in any case, the terms 'Whig' and 'Tory' were not party labels attached to opponents and supporters of the king respectively. Some of George III's ministers had called themselves Whigs. The words were more like the 'left-wing' and 'right-wing' as used today - and, of course, the words tell us more about the standpoints of people who apply them than they do about the people to whom they are applied.

There is no denying that Namier's approach involved detailed, card-index style, research. One can certainly see why he was hailed as 'Britain's answer to Leopold von Ranke'. And, as Linda Colley[13] points out, he sometimes saw himself in the mould of the objective researcher into the documents of past politics. The word 'Namierisation' was coined - and indeed entered the Oxford English Dictionary - to refer to exact and detailed scholarship. But, as with Ranke himself, the truth is more complex. We need to look very carefully at the type of source most frequently used by Namier to understand his approach. Faced with letters and memoirs, Namier was in his element. The more personal the source, the better he liked it and the more exhaustively he used it. The link with prosopography is clear. But the question is - why this interest in this type of source? In short, he was fascinated by the individual in history because he was obsessed by his own psyche, scarred as it was by the many contradictions of his life. Born Ludwik Bernsztajn vel Niemirowski in Galicia, eastern Poland, his parents were Jews, but did not practise their religion. His native tongue should have been Ukrainian, but his parents tried to stop him from speaking it on the grounds that it was inappropriate for those who wished truly to belong to the landed élites of Poland. He stood to inherit his father's lands and had the tastes and outlook of an aristocrat, but was disinherited. He became a British subject in 1913, having emerged from Balliol College, Oxford with a first-class degree and a profound, quasi-mystical belief in the values and outlook of the British aristocracy. But he was too talkative, too sharp, too arrogant, too self-tormented and - given an undercurrent of anti-Semitism - too Jewish, to be accepted into the ranks of the élites. Despite his evident abilities and growing academic reputation, he failed to secure fellowships or chairs at either Oxford or Cambridge. His attempts to come to terms with his Jewishness led him to work with zeal for the Zionist Organisation whose aim was to establish a Jewish homeland in Palestine: his craving for acceptance into the world of the British establishment led him to hope (against all reason) that such a state would be part of the British Empire. He then proceeded to alienate his Jewish friends by converting to Anglicanism in 1947. Namier, then, was the quintessential outsider whose quest for self-identity led him to sink himself into obsessive work and onto the couches of the psychoanalysts.

Namier approached the writing of history with a belief that what shaped the past was political behaviour, and that what shaped political behaviour was human nature. Ideas were a potent force, but ideas were adopted not because human beings calmly and rationally selected the ones appropriate to their needs: they were adopted at an instinctive and emotional level. It was this level, he felt, which must concern the historian. This meant that an ideology such as communism could hold few attractions for him, even beyond his landowner's distaste for the urban masses. He denied the truth of any system based on an appeal to reason and a promise of progress, since, in so doing, it failed to take into account the troubled human psyche. The one intellectual system which did allegedly base itself on the workings of the psyche was Freudian psychoanalysis - of which Namier had personal experience. It explained for Namier not only his own personality - in particular, his conflict with his father - but it also gave him the approach he needed to study history: namely, at the level of the individual and the group. In effect, he was being offered the chance of writing himself into his history and history into himself, and who could resist such a temptation?

The flaws in Namier's work are a reflection of his virtues. As John Cannon has pointed out[14], Namier's books are ill-structured: minute analysis of archival material and prosopography are hard to integrate into any form of narrative. Namier was a fine stylist, and found his inability to make his work flow for the reader deeply frustrating. His Freudianism led to often illuminating discussions of the background and motivations of his characters, but also to a tendency to concentrate on those who were clearly neurotic: or, if they were not so clearly neurotic, then Namier found a suitable neurosis for them. It was helpful to be reminded of the extent to which human behaviour was affected by impulse and emotion, but less helpful to be informed that impulse and emotion are virtually all there is. In a lecture to the British Academy in 1944, Namier commented on the contribution of the German populace in the revolution of 1848:

> The mob had come out in revolt, moved by passions and distress rather than ideas: they had no articulate aims, and no one will ever be able to supply a rational explanation of what it was they fought for, or what made them fight.

To dismiss the influence of ideas on human conduct in this way is simplistic and scarcely reflects Namier's own experience. His attachment to his particular brand of Zionism was surely more than the product of his own psyche.

And finally, there is something contradictory in what Namier was doing. He was refusing to accept the validity of patterns, theories and models in history, and yet was imposing on history his own understanding of Freud, whose writings he treated as if they had established incontrovertible laws. To do so meant that he was projecting onto history the view that human nature was unchanging at the level of emotions, instincts and feelings: a procedure which at least lays itself open to the danger of anachronism. Like Butterfield, Namier had not left the Whigs behind in his own work.

Namier's impact on the writing of history outside Britain was negligible, but inside the country, immense. Richard Evans comments:

> When I was an undergraduate in the 1960s, Namier's *Structure of Politics* was considered by history tutors to have been the greatest work ever penned about English history, and Namier was a god.[15]

He was a god because he was, it seemed, providing a technique which raised historical scholarship to new levels. Such precision, such detail, such exactitude, such relentless dismissing of all-encompassing theories about progress: Namier was supposedly offering to his followers the mantle of true objectivity and a recognition of the value of the individual. This mantle was well worth having as a protection against the claims of one's Marxist opponents across the Cold War divide. And yet, as we have seen, using Namier in this way is to distort him, just as Ranke was distorted by his followers. The extent to which his work was the product of his own tortured life and obsession with Freud was all but ignored.

The impact of both Butterfield and Namier was to confirm the pre-existing tendencies of British historiography towards the Rankean empiricist (roughly, one who works not on the basis of theory but through observation and evidence). It is scarcely to be denied that a kind of bastardised Rankeanism dominated - perhaps still dominates - academic history in Europe and North America. Assumptions about what makes a good historian are very often based on methodology derived ultimately from Ranke. That supposed mark of entry into the profession of history, the PhD, generally remains a heavily-detailed and narrow discussion based largely on original sources.

It is also scarcely to be denied that bastardised Rankeanism led to a restricted subject-matter for history. The Rankean approach brought the shutters down on the very Enlightenment historiography which was expanding the concerns of the historian into the areas of social history (particularly, as we have seen, customs and manners) and economic history. We recall that it was not as if Ranke was uninterested in these areas, but rather that his sources and his views on the God-given national spirit led him into political and military history. Many of his successors lacked even that interest.

The Rankean, anti-whig style of history can be criticised because it fights shy of evaluating development through time. Studying development need not necessarily be judgemental, and, even when there appears to be a definite line of progress from past towards the present (as in the history of science), then the good historian can still evaluate those who did not contribute towards progress in the context of their own times and with fairness.

To deny to history the right to study development causes other potential problems. As we shall see in the concluding chapter, the fundamental human need to understand the present requires an understanding of the past and how the past shaped the present. If historians refuse to help provide it, then others who are less qualified will. The dangers of allowing them to do so are very real (see pages 146-147). There are certainly those who would argue that to deny a link between historical study and present politics and society is, ultimately, a dangerous dereliction of duty. Memorably, Pieter Geyl, writing in the aftermath of his experiences in the hands of Nazis in his native Holland, commented that:

> Historicism, in the sense of an interpretation of history which acknowl-
> edges no standards outside the object, is abhorrent to me ... a disin-
> terested understanding of what is alien to you - this is not the function
> of the mind which will supply the most trenchant weapons for the polit-
> 5 ical rough-and-tumble.[16]

And yet, Geyl also offers an eloquent testimony to the lasting appeal of impartiality and objectivity. Geyl argues that, as they are essential parts of liberal culture - an academic version of fair play - their seductiveness is very real. After all, the opposite could easily be seen as bigotry or arrogance. This is why Geyl suddenly stops dead in his tracks:

> Yet how admirable, nevertheless, is that serene matter-of-factness, that
> striving after comprehension, that openmindedness ... qualities which
> have had a broadening effect on nineteenth-century civilisation and
> which (need I remind you?) are the complete opposite of the revolu-
> 5 tionary fanaticism and doctrinairism of the men who half a century after
> his [Ranke's] death threw Germany and the world into the catastrophe
> ... To understand is a function of the mind that not only enriches the
> life of the individual but is the very breath of the civilisation we are
> called to defend.[17]

14 Conclusion

This chapter has offered a focus on two historians whose attitudes and approaches seem miles apart. Gibbon, as a representative of the Enlightenment, wrote in a spirit which was judgemental. He felt equipped to make such judgements because he saw human nature as constant through time and because he felt that he had escaped from the intellectual chains of organised religion. Ranke hated this. The *philosophes* were, in his view, irreligious and arrogant and no respecters of history, which they distorted to fit their own theories. Each age was unique, and not to be hijacked by those who loved it only in so far as it provided evidence for their own meaningless system-building. History was to be studied on its own terms and for its own sake through the strenuous and impartial efforts of the historian.

Of course, digging deeper into the work of Gibbon and Ranke has revealed a complexity which, to my mind, is more stimulating than the generalisations above, however useful they may be as starting points. We had reason to suggest that the Enlightenment was by no means a unified movement, and that Gibbon himself was dismissive of his fellow *philosophes* for their failure to respect the canons of historical proof. Ranke's subject-matter was chosen in part because he hoped to reveal, however vaguely, the footsteps of God in history. Ironically, although Ranke developed a more sophisticated historical technique and emphasised the use of original documents, his work has been superseded: Gibbon's factual accuracy remains largely unimpeached.

Digging also revealed surprising resemblances. We dismissed the familiar charge that Gibbon's style was an end in itself, and argued that it operated as a way of pulling the reader into the mind of the historian and, in the creative dialogue that ensued, potentially encouraged a sense of empathy. Despite expectations to the contrary, Ranke's style was not bare and unadorned, but exploited effectively a range of literary devices because he believed that letting the past speak could and should be an emotional and spiritual experience.

Without a doubt, it is Ranke who made the greater contribution to the development of historiography. But we noted that his successors frequently distorted, in their quest for an allegedly 'scientific' history, Ranke's own work. The narrow specialism of the PhD is certainly a product of the Rankean emphasis on scholarly technique and archival research, but it bears little resemblance to the wide-ranging narrative histories written by Ranke himself. Similarly, Ranke has often been criticised for diverting history into the restrictions of politics and grand diplomacy, whereas the philosophic historians were interested in a far greater range - including culture, manners and laws. This is unfair, in the sense that Ranke was interested in many aspects of history but was led by the nature of his available sources and the sheer scale of his work to focus on political history. It is not his fault that his legacy - as misinterpreted by his followers - was indeed to restrict the scope of history.

Finally, I would like to think that this relatively detailed discussion of Gibbon and Ranke has raised some issues which are as relevant today as they were then. Just how far, for example, is the historian to seek to engage the reader in his work? Is objectivity a goal which must dominate the thinking of the historian, or is it a necessary first step, allowing the historian the right to then make value-judgements?

References
1   G.R. Elton, *The Practice of History* (Fontana, 1969), p. 14.
2   Arnaldo Momigliano, *Studies in Historiography* (Garland, 1966), p. 40.
3   J.W. Burrows, *Gibbon* (Oxford University Press, 1985).

4   John Clive, *Not by Fact Alone. Essays on the Writing and Reading of History* (Collins Harvill, 1990).
5   G.G. Iggers and Konrad von Moltke (eds.), *The Theory and Practice of History* (Bobbs-Merrill, 1973). A useful collection of short extracts from Ranke on the study and writing of history.
6   Ibid., pp. xix-xx.
7   Ibid., p. lix.
8   Gino Benzoni, in G.G. Iggers and J.M. Powell (eds.), *Leopold von Ranke and the Shaping of the Historical Discipline,* (Syracuse University Press, 1990) pp. 45-57.
9   Peter Gay, *Style in History* (Cape, 1975), p. 62.
10 Owen Dudley Edwards, *Macaulay* (Weidenfeld & Nicolson, 1988), p. 126.
11 J.H. Plumb, *The Death of the Past* (Macmillan, 1969), p. 42.
12 R.H.C. Davies, 'The Content of History', *History* LXVI (1981), p. 364.
13 Linda Colley, *Namier* (Weidenfeld & Nicolson, 1989), pp. 21-2.
14 John Cannon (ed.), *The Historian at Work* (Allen & Unwin, 1980), pp. 136-153.
15 R.J. Evans, *In Defence of History* (Granta, 1997), pp. 33-4.
16 Pieter Geyl, *Debates with Historians* (Fontana, 1962), pp. 28-9.
17 Ibid., p. 29.

Making notes on 'From the Enlightenment of the Eighteenth century to Leopold von Ranke and the Rankean Tradition'

As in previous chapters, I suggest that note-making is based around the following summary diagram. Make sure you provide yourself with one or two memorable quotations from Gibbon with which to impress the examiner. And do not forget to refer explicitly to his works by exact title: examiners are constantly depressed by the inability of candidates to offer this most minimal of courtesies.

Summary Diagram
From the Enlightenment to Leopold von Ranke

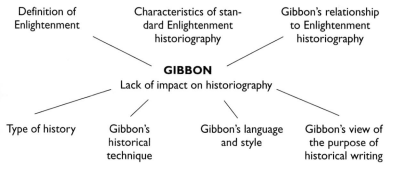

Summary Diagram
From the Enlightenment to Leopold von Ranke

Reasons for Ranke's dislike of Enlightenemt historiography

Ranke's historical technique

Type of history

Ranke's language and style

RANKE
Impact on historiography

Butterfield's attack on Whig history

Namier

Answering essay questions on 'From the Enlightenment of the Eighteenth century to Leopold von Ranke and the Rankean Tradition'

This chapter offers plenty of scope for comparison questions based on the characteristics of historians. A typical question might focus on one quality, but nevertheless would definitely require a discussion of other qualities as well. For example:

1. 'The most important attribute of an historian is an effective style.' Comment on this view, with particular reference to the work of at least two historians.
2. 'The most important attribute of an historian is factual accuracy, acquired through strict objectivity.' Comment on this view, with particular reference to the work of at least two historians.

These questions certainly lend themselves to a comparison of Gibbon and Ranke, although one would hope that you could refer to other historians mentioned in this chapter. Ask yourself how references to Macaulay, Butterfield and Namier might complement your argument in either or both of these questions.

Making a plan for an essay, you will recall, is the vital process through which you identify key words and the relevant material; it also allows you to get your argument clear in your mind and to make decisions about what evidence it is relevant to include. Have a go at creating a plan for question 2, and then write the introductory paragraph of your essay.

There are clear opportunities for the confident candidate to bring in a brief assessment of the postmodern perspective on objectivity (as in Chapter 5). This would be very impressive when used within a conclusion to provide a broader context.

In both Chapter 2 and Chapter 3, it was suggested that you could, with benefit, use Ranke in a question on contribution to the development of historiography. Try writing both a plan and an opening statement of argument for question 3.

3. Discuss the contribution to the development of historical writing of Leopold von Ranke.

It is important that you remember to put Ranke into the context of the *philosophes,* since his impact not only helped to shape subsequent historiography but also had the effect of halting in its tracks Enlightenment historiography. The general rule for tackling this kind of question is to organise your answer in two sections - one on the effect of the historian on his contemporary scene, and the second on his legacy.

Source-based questions on 'From the Enlightenment of the Eighteenth century to Leopold von Ranke and the Rankean Tradition'

1. Extracts from Gibbon
a) Read the extract on Pope John XII (page 53). What attitudes typical of the *philosophe* are demonstrated by Gibbon? (3 marks)
b) What characteristics of Gibbon as an historian are shown by the extracts on page 53 and pages 53-54 (on Ladislaus and Origen)? (7 marks)

2. Extracts from Leopold von Ranke
a) Read the extract on page 59. (from Ranke's preface). What do Ranke's words tell you about his view of the proper writing of history? (5 marks)
b) Write a critical evaluation of Acton's comments on Ranke on page 65. (5 marks)

Question 2b) gives you an excellent opportunity to offer a balanced argument. Acton has, after all, not got it completely wrong. Remember to put Acton into his own context: what was he looking for in Ranke?

4 From Karl Marx to the Annales School

1 Karl Marx and Marxism

Karl Marx (1818-83) was a contemporary of Ranke, also had a lawyer for a father and was nurtured, like him, in German culture at a German university. He too had a major impact on historiography in his own country and beyond which very much persists to this day. But there the similarities end. Marx was not an historian as such, detested German nationalism, saw religion as a cause of man's alienation from himself and from his society and spent a considerable part of his adult life an exile from his own country. To Marx, the great shaping force of the nineteenth century was not the Rankean mix of nationalism, the power of the state, the politics of the élites and behind them all the barely-detectable workings of God: it was the bitter drama of industrialization and the dominance of capitalism. And finally, Marx wanted and expected his ideas to change the world (and they did): to Ranke, this would seem to be godless presumption.

In 1843, after concluding his doctoral thesis at the University of Berlin and working as a journalist, Marx moved to Paris, where he found himself in the congenial - if quarrelsome - company of progressive thinkers. By 1844, he had met Friedrich Engels who, despite (or because of) being the son of an industrialist, was a revolutionary socialist. Both Marx and Engels were more than happy to be labelled Communists and got themselves commissioned by the congress (in London) of a new organisation called the Communist League to produce a pamphlet explaining the League's stance in a straightforward form. And so, Marx and Engels' *The Communist Manifesto* was published in February 1848. According to Engels' preface to the English edition of 1888, its fundamental thesis originated from Marx: namely, that the whole history of mankind was a history of struggles between classes in societies which were shaped by the 'prevailing mode of economic production'. The publication of the *Manifesto* had nothing to do with the outburst of revolutions in a number of European countries later that year, but the failure of those revolutions meant that Marx fled to London in August 1849. There, he spent the rest of his life: partly supported by Engels, partly by journalism and partly due to fortunate legacies to his wife, Jenny. In 1867, he completed the first volume of his massive work *Capital*, but his work *The Civil War in France* (1871) (about the contemporary and unsuccessful workers' uprising, the Paris Commune) brought him more immediate recognition as a communist thinker. His personal political influence over such communist organisations as the First International was, however, limited. It was left to Engels to fan the flame of Marx's ideas, and the twentieth century, particularly through the communist revolutions in Russia in 1917 and in Mao's

China after 1949, to claim them as inspiration for a new world order.

And yet, how times change. In the 1990s, States officially subscribing to the ideas of Marx became increasingly few and far between. Of course, this may seem to be irrelevant to a book on historiography. But it is not. Since Marx's ideas on the nature of history were part and parcel of his revolutionary teachings and vision of progress through time, no critique of his thought can afford to ignore relatively modern political events which might be seen as evidence of the accuracy of those ideas.

2 Marx and History: Historical Determinism

Many millions of words have been written about Marx's ideas, but before I add to their number it is best, in the standard historian's manner, to recognize the pitfalls and limitations. First of all, there is simply no single, indisputable Marxist canon (set of established principles) which allows us to say 'Yes, this is what Marx meant about history'. There are, as we shall see, possible inconsistencies and gaps in his thought as revealed in his published and unpublished writings. In fact, some of his most significant arguments can be interpreted in different ways: so much so that Engels, after Marx's death, felt obliged to comment on what Marx - in Engels' opinion - *really* meant. We shall be able to trace the varied interpretations of Marx in the differing use to which his ideas were put by historians.

Let us start by taking a key passage from *A Contribution to the Critique of Political Economy* (1859) in which Marx explained the genesis of his ideas.

1 The general conclusion at which I arrived and which, once reached, continued to serve as the leading thread in my studies may be briefly summed up as follows: in the social production which men carry on they enter into definite relations that are indispensable and independent of
5 their will; these relations of production correspond to a definite stage of development of their material powers of production. The sum total of these relations of production constitute the economic structure of society - the real foundation, on which rise legal and political superstructures and to which correspond definite forms of social conscious-
10 ness. The mode of production in material life determines the general character of the social, political, and spiritual processes of life. It is not the consciousness of men that determines their existence, but, on the contrary, their social existence determines their consciousness. At a certain stage of their development the material forces of production in
15 society come into conflict with the existing relations of production, or - what is but a legal expression for the same thing - with the property relations within which they had been at work before. From forms of development of the forces of production these relations turn into their fetters. Then comes the period of social revolution. With the change of

20 the economic foundation the entire immense superstructure is more or
less rapidly transformed. In considering such transformations the
distinction should always be made between the material transformation
of the economic conditions of production, which can be determined
25 with the precision of natural science, and the legal, political, religious,
aesthetic, or philosophic - in short, ideological - forms in which men
become conscious of this conflict and fight it out.

Let us see if we can unravel Marx's ideas and put them in a more
straightforward way. First, there is a label (provided by Engels) to
attach to his fundamental approach: *historical materialism.* This means
that economic (material) conditions shape everything significant in
human society. So, change in history must come about because of
changes in economic conditions. It is vital to understand the importance of this point. Marx spoke of 'material powers of production' (or
'productive forces', as he often terms it) and 'relations of production'. Productive forces are simply those things needed to produce
the food and the goods required by a given society, such as technology
and tools, the raw material and the labour needed to use them. The
relations of production are the relations (generally between classes of
people, or a relationship between a person and property) which make
that production happen - such as factory boss and worker, landlord
and tenant, noble and serf, owning, renting, wage-earning. Marx
argued that relations of production must correspond to (and be
shaped by) the powers of production. He put this with a kind of brutal
simplicity in *The Poverty of Philosophy* (1847) where he said:

> The handmill gives you society with the feudal lord; the steam mill,
> society with the industrial capitalist.

Marx added that the economic base or foundation of society rests
upon these relations of production. Crucially, he argued that all the
visible aspects of society - its superstructure above these foundations
- are shaped by the relations of production. So, our political institutions, our legal systems, our religious beliefs, our value-systems, our
media, our ideologies, our educational institutions, are determined
by the economic base: hence the phrase often used to describe this
theory - economic determinism. In other words, what we are in any
given society is shaped by economic relationships. We might assume
that we can come up with political ideas just by inspiration or
abstract theorizing, but they are, in fact, the creation of that
economic base. This is why Marx talked of the consciousness of men
being created by their social existence, rather than the consciousness of men creating that social existence.

Perhaps an example would help. We can take the time of the
'steam mill and the industrial capitalist' and see how Marx's concept
of the base-superstructure applies. The economic base rests upon
the relations of production, which are - in Marx's terminology - the

bourgeoisie, or middle-class property-owners, led by industrial capitalists, who control and exploit for their own profit the industrial workers (the proletariat). And so, all the visible aspects of society serve the needs of this relationship - dominated, as it is, by the bourgeoisie. The political system which suits the bourgeoisie is parliamentary democracy, because this takes power away from the feudal landowning classes and monarchs but does not give it directly to the workers. In the nineteenth century, few workers had the vote anyway. The religious values also serve the needs of this relationship, because Christianity is used by the bourgeoisie to encourage deference (respect for and trust in one's superiors) among the workers and to distract them from their sufferings and exploitation on earth by offering the rewards of Heaven. The education system is geared to the needs of industry, aiming to turn out deferential workers with appropriate skills or middle-class entrepreneurs with a competitive spirit. Perhaps an imaginary conversation might make the complex arguments clearer.

Nineteenth-Century British Mill Owner

I feel in my conscience that I should do something for my workers. Does the Bible not say that I must help my neighbour? I would be shirking my God-given responsibility if I did not try to educate my workers, to curb their gin-drinking and their vicious lives. I will build them decent housing, close the public houses and give them rational forms of entertainment.

Marxist Response

How convenient. You say your ideas are shaped by the promptings of God within your soul and your study of the Bible. They are actually shaped by your economic need. What you want is a skilled workforce, so you educate them. You want them to be disciplined and punctual, so you build decent houses near to the factory and stop their traditional customs and visits to the inns. You may not realise it, but your religion is just a cloak for your class interest. I suppose they will be persuaded to go to chapel, where your preacher will encourage them to be deferential and hard-working in God's name.

Now, what did Marx mean when he talked about the period of social revolution, when the productive forces come into conflict with the relations of production? Let us take the feudal period, characterised by hand or horse-powered technology and static relationships between a land-owning aristocracy and a land-less peasantry. But productive forces start developing - the machine-age dawns. Steam power demands factories and towns (so that large numbers of workers can live near their places of employment), but landowners try to preserve the old ways. So conflict arises with the growing capitalist class of the bourgeoisie as they create the new relations of production (factory-owner and worker) demanded by the new productive forces. As part of the process, the old relations of production of the landowner/serf variety try and fail to hold back the developing productive forces of capitalism. Marx suggested a contradiction (the philosophical term is a *dialectic*) between the relations of production and forces of production: this leads to major historical change. *Dialectical materialism* is the term normally used to describe this portion of Marx's thinking. In his use of the dialectic, we see Marx's adaptation of the thought of the philosopher Hegel, who saw in ideas the motive force behind history. Each age, according to Hegel, was characterized by a dominant idea (or thesis) which nevertheless contained within itself a directly opposing idea (or antithesis). From the resulting contradiction and conflict (the dialectic) came a new synthesis - itself, of course, the dominant idea of the next age. As a materialist, Marx was replacing the concept of the dominant idea with the economic base.

There are three important points to make here. Firstly, it seems that Marx claimed that the economic transformations he had identified had the status of laws explaining the workings of nature. Secondly, it is clear that Marx offered a fundamental structure to history, based upon the forces and relations of production (which taken together he termed 'modes of production'). These modes of production were, in order, Asiatic, ancient, feudal and capitalist. And thirdly, Marx attached considerable importance to social classes - feudal, bourgeois, proletarian - within that structure. To help us with the two last points, I need to refer in some detail to the *Communist Manifesto*.

1   The history of all society up to now is the history of class struggles.
    Freeman and slave, patrician and plebeian, lord and serf ... in short,
    oppressor and oppressed stood in continual conflict with one another
    ... a struggle that finished each time with a revolutionary transforma-
5   tion of society as a whole, or with the common ruin of the contending
    classes ...

Marx continued by arguing that the system of capitalism, like the system of feudalism before it, brings about its own destruction:

1   ... with the development of industry the proletariat not only increases;
    it is forced together in greater masses, its power grows and it feels it
    more ... machinery increasingly obliterates different types of labour and
    forces wages down to an almost equally low level. The increasing
5   competition of the bourgeois amongst themselves and the crises
    emerging therefrom make the worker's wage ever more fluctuating ...

However, class conflict was, in Marx's view, by no means never-ending. The proletariat would indeed overthrow the bourgeoisie and, through using the State as its instrument of control, would transform the relations of production by abolishing private ownership and therefore class conflict for ever. And, since human characteristics like greed and lust for personal property are not innate but the products of a particular economic base, then co-operation would replace competition and the State would simply dissolve. With the disappearance of class conflict, there would be no further need for State control.

What Marx is doing is offering a new periodisation of history based on changes in productive forces and also - crucially - a projection into the future. The basic outline of his theories is, I hope, reasonably clear, but there are aspects of it which are problematic. As presented so far, it seems to be rigidly determinist: productive forces shape relations of production and the resulting economic base of society shapes its ideologies, political and legal structures and so on. So, there seems to be no place for the human free will, or ideas developing independently of the base. This seems most unlikely. Are we really to accept the view that religious belief - or ethics, for that matter - are simply the product of the economic base? It is difficult to see how those who have sacrificed everything for an ideal do so for reasons which are concealed - perhaps even to them.

In any case, if political ideas are not genuine agents of change, why should Marx devote so much time to political organizations? Why not simply await the death of capitalism, which came from within? As Peter Singer puts it:

> … if neither thought nor politics has any real causal significance, what is the meaning of Marx's dedication, intellectually and politically, to the cause of the working class?[1]

3 Marx and Determinism

I have suggested that crude economic determinism would appear to be a relatively easy target. But, despite the evidence from the *Critique of Political Economy* (and from several other of Marx's comments), it is possible to argue that Marx did not intend to claim that the superstructure could not affect the base, and so deny that political or religious ideas had their effect on the mode of production. After Marx's death, Engels claimed that neither he nor Marx had ever taught an iron law of economic determinism. In one letter of 1890, Engels wrote:

1 According to the materialist conception of history, the *ultimately* determining element in history is the production and reproduction of real life. More than this neither Marx nor I have ever asserted. Hence if somebody twists this into saying that the economic element is the *only*
5 determining one he transforms that proposition into a meaningless, abstract, senseless, phrase. The economic situation is the basis, but the

various elements of the superstructure ... also exercise their influence upon the course of the historical struggles and in many cases preponderate in determining their *form*. There is an interaction of all these
10   elements in which, amidst all the endless host of accidents ... the economic movement finally asserts itself as necessary ... Marx and I are ourselves partly to blame for the fact that the younger people sometimes lay more stress on the economic side than is due to it.

I hope I am not the only one to find Engels' meaning a little elusive here. He appears to be arguing that elements of the superstructure - let us assume political ideas - can in some way affect the base. But he then argues that, in some unspecified way, the economic element 'finally asserts itself as necessary' - presumably meaning that, in the end, society *is* determined by economics.

This 'ultimately deterministic' stance does appear to be reflected in some of Marx's writings, although some historians have downplayed the extent to which Marx was determinist at all. To discuss this problematic issue further, I want in particular to look at Marx's *Eighteenth Brumaire of Louis Bonaparte* (1852). I have chosen this particular work because it is an excellent example of Marx writing contemporary history and because some scholars use it to argue that determinism was not an essential ingredient of Marx's thought.

Louis Bonaparte was a nephew of the great Napoleon and had been elected President of the French Republic established after the overthrow of the King, Louis Philippe, in 1848. In 1851, Bonaparte staged a coup, overthrew the Republic and was proclaimed Emperor. Marx's title, the 'eighteenth brumaire', is an ironic reference to the coup staged by the first Napoleon - an incomparably more impressive figure than his nephew. Now, one can admire Marx for tackling this subject, because it appeared to run counter to his class struggle analysis. It was undeniable that Louis Napoleon was supported by considerable numbers of the bourgeoisie and some of the workers in defiance, it would seem, of their class interests. After all, the Marxist model would suggest that the middle classes would aim for a parliamentary-style democracy and the workers for state control in the name and interests of the proletariat.

The Eighteenth Brumaire is wonderfully lively and contains some splendidly vigorous attacks on the bourgeoisie and Bonaparte himself. Marx offers a detailed political analysis of the complex events and interest-groups and seems to take into account the effect of Bonaparte's personality and cunning on what happened - perhaps not the most obvious line of attack if one were to expect historical determinism and class struggle analysis. But, having said all this, I would argue that *The Eighteenth Brumaire* is firmly anchored in economic determinism. For example, when discussing the different factions amongst the pro-royalists, Marx remarked:

> 1   What kept the two factions apart was not any so-called principles, it was
>   their material conditions of existence ... On the different forms of
>   property, the social conditions of existence, arises an entire superstruc-
>   ture of different and peculiarly formed sentiments, delusions, modes of
> 5   thought and outlooks on life. The whole class creates and forms them
>   from the material foundations on up ...

So, *The Eighteenth Brumaire* rests upon economic determinism as expressed through its class-based analysis: an analysis which does not dominate the content in a blunt and unsophisticated way, but which very much reflects Engels' view that, ultimately, it is the economic base which counts.

One final point on the issue of economic determinism. Let us look at the implications of accepting (however tentatively) Engels' argument that he and Marx were agreed that elements of the superstructure might influence in some way the base, but that, in the end, the base remained the real shaper of history. The problem is simply stated: what does 'in the end' mean? It is difficult to see how one can accept a reciprocal (two-way) action between base and superstructure but also insist that, ultimately, the base is more important. In what circumstances? Or in every circumstance? Partial determinism seems like a contradiction in terms.

Of course, it could be argued that what matters is not so much how determinist Marx was than how the issue of economic determinism affected historians influenced by Marx. This issue is explored in the next section.

4 The Impact of Marx on Historiography

There are really three ways in which Marx's ideas might have an impact on historiography. The first is when a country becomes communist and upholds Marxism as the political, philosophical and historical truth. The second is where historians in a non-communist country are themselves communist. The third is the possible influence of Marxist historiography on non-communist historians in a non-communist country.

As one would expect, historical materialism became the official history of the communist states of Europe. And, generally speaking, where the historians of these countries were subject to the greatest degree of Party and State control (such as in the former East Germany and the USSR), then rigid economic determinism - sometimes called 'crude' or 'vulgar' Marxism by its opponents - was expected and imposed. This meant that it was accepted that Marx's view of the periodisation of history and the crude base-superstructure model had the status of natural laws, and therefore any work of history utilizing them did not need to offer balanced arguments and supporting evidence in their justification. The history of the working classes was, of course, a feature one would expect from Marxist historiography, but, in the official histories, it tended to be distorted into an institutional history concentrating on the deeds and thoughts of party leaders - so serving the ruling party's political needs.

What of the communist historians in the non-communist countries? To make this issue manageable, it might be best to take one case-study, and my choice would be the work of the British Marxist historians from the period of the setting up of the British Communist Party's Historians' Group in the aftermath of the Second World War. There are a number of reasons for this choice. A significant number of the historians associated with this group are generally accepted as fine practitioners of their discipline even by those who do not accept their political views. Their work has, at the very least, been impossible to ignore. Christopher Hill, George Rudé, E.P. Thompson and Eric Hobsbawm, amongst others, spring immediately to mind. Secondly, I have been able to take advantage of the work in this field of Harvey Kaye, whose desire to appropriate such historians for his own brand of democratic socialism has by no means compromised the value of such books as *The British Marxist Historians* and *The Education of Desire*. And finally, the British Marxist historians have much to say on the relationship between Marxist historiography and economic determinism.

Eric Hobsbawm has commented that, before the Historians' Group, there had been 'no tradition of Marxist history in Britain'.[2] For radical members of the student generation of the 1930s, communism and Marxism had many attractions. The Wall St Crash of 1929 had shaken confidence in capitalism, and, given the weak-willed response of the western democracies towards Hitler, Soviet Russia appeared to represent the only meaningful alternative to the growing power of fascism. The uncharacteristically harsh tone of Christopher Hill's short work *The English Revolution 1640*, which first appeared in 1940, can be taken to reflect a deep sense of anger at the West's failure to stand up to Hitler and to prevent a world war. The Historians' Group was formally established in 1946, and Hobsbawm speaks with affection of the sense of intellectual excitement and commitment to the cause at this time:

> Our work as historians was therefore embedded in our work as Marxists, which we believed to imply membership of the Communist Party.[3]

However, the events of 1956 broke the unity of the group. In that year, the Russian leader Khrushchev launched an attack on his feared predecessor Stalin and the excesses of Stalinism at the Congress of the Communist Party of the Soviet Union. But the British Communist Party failed to respond to it, and also failed to condemn the Russian invasion of Hungary later in the year. The result was a mass exodus from the Party, and the Historians' Group was similarly hit. Although Hobsbawm remained, Hill and Thompson were among those who left. Even so, this should not be taken as a sign that their commitment to Marxism itself had changed in any way.

I now want to look at the way in which the British Marxist historians responded to the issue of economic determinism. Here is Hobsbawm, referring to the work of the Historians' Group:

> A third advantage of our Marxism - we owe it largely to Hill and to the very marked interest of several of our members ... was never to reduce history to a simple economic or 'class interest' determinism, or to devalue politics and ideology.[4]

It seems, then, that one should not expect from the most influential British Marxist historians a crude economic determinism, but instead that factors usually referred to as part of the superstructure can be derived independently of the base and themselves affect it in some way. Is this interpretation justified when we look at their work? By and large, it is. Of course, one can point to exceptions. Hill's early essay on the English Revolution presents a simplistic explanation of it as a class war led by the bourgeois Parliament against the essentially feudal classes of monarch and major landowners - a war in which religious ideas are seen as the cloak for class interests:

> 1 ... those who wanted to overthrow the feudal state had to attack and seize control of the Church. That is why political theories tended to get wrapped up in religious language ... But the fact that men spoke and wrote in religious language should not prevent us realising that there is
> 5 a social content behind what are apparently purely theological ideas. Each class created and sought to impose the religious outlook best suited to its own needs and interests. But the real clash is between these class interests: behind the parson stood the squire.

The later Hill would be less ready to label the landowning classes as essentially feudal and much less ready to present arguments with a minimum of supporting evidence in references. Now, it is the contention of Kaye[5] - and I accept his argument - that Hill's later work retains the view that the English Revolution was bourgeois, but in the sense that its outcome favoured the development of capitalism, rather than being a revolution caused by capitalism. Kaye also points to other key developments or changes of emphasis. In his later work, Hill is keen to stress (and demonstrate in his work) that it is wrong to limit an analysis of class to economics, or to see ideas as the product of economic circumstances in a simplistic way. In *The Intellectual Origins of the English Revolution* (1965), Hill comments:

> Marx himself did not fall into the error of thinking that men's ideas were merely a pale reflection of their economic needs, with no history of their own; but some of his successors ... have been more economic-determinist than Marx.

Despite such comments about crude base-superstructure Marxism, it is clear that Hill still accepts class-struggle as central to the process of history. The marked characteristic of much of Hill's more recent work has been a mastery of an extraordinary quantity and range of written sources as he places the emphasis on the significance of culture to class-struggle analysis. Culture is, of course, not to be seen as the mere product of economic relationships. This is clearly stated in Hill's 1989 book *A Turbulent, Seditious and Factious People: John Bunyan and his Church*. In seeking the answer to the question of why changes took place in popular culture in early modern Europe, Hill comments:

I Phrases like 'the rise of individualism','of capitalism' are groping towards an answer, but a merely economic definition is too narrow. For England our answer must include - among many other things - an explanation of the decline of magic, of hell, of Calvinism as a dominant intellectual system …

Even so, I can see no evidence that Hill is rejecting the *primacy* of material factors in class-struggle analysis. After all, he talks of the economic definition being too narrow, rather than inappropriate. And, in 'A Bourgeois Revolution', he significantly defines a class as the position its members have in relation to other classes and to the *productive process*: in other words, a definition which offers a fundamentally economic basis for class. Elsewhere, Hill comments that historians of culture need economic history, 'because culture is a class phenomenon.' So, to study class, economic history appears to have primacy of place, even if it is not the only significant factor.

This has been a complex discussion, but a necessary one. What we seem to see in Hill is a Marxist whose early polemic (controversial work) *The English Revolution 1640*, with its rather crude, relatively unsupported economic determinism focused on causes, has been replaced by work of far greater sophistication, in which the bourgeois revolution thesis is redirected at the consequences of the revolution. Hill does not accept the vulgar Marxist view that the superstructure is entirely the product of the economic base. But I believe there remains a commitment to economic determinism, even though that commitment is worn rather lightly as Hill pursues his interest in studying class-struggle through culture. I recall hearing Hill say that his vocabulary had changed since his earliest published work, but that his ideas were really the same. His stance, in fact, is not dissimilar to that of Engels. Hill faces, perhaps, the same problem as other Marxists who accept a two-way action between base and superstructure: to what extent can the superstructure really affect the base when economic factors are the vital ingredient?

Hill's approach to Marxism is paralleled in the work of other former members of the Historians' Group. E.P. Thompson's *The Making of the English Working Class* (1963) offers an approach to class which is openly critical of those who write as if the working classes were created purely by the productive processes of the Industrial Revolution. The danger is that the workers will be seen merely as data, as examples to prove a point, if the historian does not consider how the workers actually handle those experiences and try to interpret them in terms of their traditions and existing values (or culture). Thompson is keen - even desperate - to ensure that any definition of class allows for the contribution and experience of real human beings, not merely the responses of someone who matters only because he is representative of a particular class. After all, Thompson's involvement in contemporary politics (particularly with CND, the Campaign for Nuclear Disarmament) must surely imply that change can take place through the actions of ordinary people. As with his politics, so with his history. Thompson duly makes his case for writing about the working classes:

1 I am seeking to rescue the poor stockinger, the Luddite cropper, the 'obsolete' hand-loom weaver, the 'utopian' artisan ... from the enormous condescension of posterity. Their crafts and traditions may have been dying. Their hostility to the new industrialism may have been back-
5 ward-looking. Their communitarian ideals may have been fantasies. Their insurrectionary conspiracies may have been foolhardy. But they lived through these times of acute social disturbance, and we did not. Their aspirations were valid in terms of their own experience; and, if they were casualties of history, they remain, condemned in their own lives, as
10 casualties.

This is wonderfully eloquent, but not, of course, a dismissal of economic determinism. His croppers and weavers were, after all, the victims of an Industrial Revolution which made their crafts obsolete. So, although they reacted in a way which reflected their own culture, their actual experiences are ultimately determined by the forces of production.

To conclude. Thompson's route is different from that of Hill, but the intention is similar. Both historians are ultimately unwilling to shed determinism, but are equally unwilling to see human beings as victims of historical forces rather than being responsible in some way (however limited) for their own lives. The difficulties of this stance have been the subject of the last few paragraphs (please see the 'Summary Diagram' on page 92).

What, then, do historians who are not primarily Marxist owe to Karl Marx? This question is an adaptation of a chapter title in Eric Hobsbawm's *On History*, so it seems only fair to start with Hobsbawm's comments. He himself starts by reminding us of the contribution and limitations - mainly the latter - of the Rankean tradition. In particular, professional history following Ranke tended to restrict itself to politics, war, diplomacy and the concerns of the élites. In Hobsbawm's view, Rankean-style history contributed little to the understanding of human society, past or present.

So, what type of history has Marx stimulated? It seems very obvious to say that social and economic history owes much to Marx, and this is

Summary Diagram
Marx, Economic Determinism and Marxist Historians

How fundamental is economic determinism to Marx's thought?

Fundamental	'Ultimately' / 'In the last resort'
Crude base-superstructure model. The superstructure cannot influence the base. Ideas are derived from the mode of production.	The superstructure can affect the base within limits. Ideas need not be derived from the mode of production.
Early Christopher Hill. Most old Soviet Bloc historians.	Later Christopher Hill. The other British Marxist historians.

true within limits. After all, Marx offers a way of relating economic history to social history (and to political history, for that matter) through historical materialism and class struggle. This is very seductive. In short, Marxism offers the historian not only a model on which to base his methodology, but also a purpose. As Hill puts it in a 1948 article for *The Modern Quarterly* article, 'the historian himself must have a vision of society and the social process as a whole: he must have a philosophy'. Marxism therefore makes it possible for historians to tackle some of the 'big issues' - change through time, the impact of industrialisation, the causes and effect of imperialism, political and social revolution - by offering hypotheses on what is likely to be most significant in an otherwise off-putting avalanche of historical data. One need only consider the scale and breadth of Hobsbawm's *Age of ...* books to appreciate this point: *The Age of Revolution* (1962); *The Age of Capital* (1975); *The Age of Empire* (1987). *The Making of the English Working Class* and Hill's textbook *The Century of Revolution, 1603-1714* (1961) are similarly wide-ranging and offer interpretations which subsequent historians of whatever persuasion simply cannot ignore. The relationship between Marxism and the discipline of economic history is less direct and more tenuous than one might expect. It would certainly be untrue to say that economic history owed its being to Marx. After all, the experience of the Industrial Revolution itself was likely to arouse interest in economics. This, rather than Marx, explains the growth of economic history in the USA at the end of the nineteenth century. Significantly, American economic history and mainstream history tended to drift apart - hardly a characteristic of Marxist historiography. Nor does the economic history practised in late twentieth century America owe much to Marx: the so-called New Economic History or 'cliometrics', which offers explanations based (according to one of its chief practitioners, Fogel) on 'explicit behavioural models ... and quantitative evidence'[6] rather than on class struggle and historical materialism.

Marxist class analysis has, as we have seen, helped to stimulate an interest in cultural history. In particular, the study of popular culture has increasingly developed into an accepted branch of academic history since the late 1970s. This is not to say that those involved in the study of popular culture owe their discipline or methodology purely to Marx. Interest in popular culture was a feature of growing nationalism in Europe in the late eighteenth and nineteenth centuries and, if we look at it historiographically, then the dissatisfaction with traditional, event-based political and diplomatic history was not restricted to Marxists. In any case, those who now study popular culture are as likely to be influenced by the French *Annales* school (whose origins owe little to Marxism - see pages 95-96) and/or anthropology as they are by Hill, Thompson or Marxist theoreticians.

One area where Marxist influences are more clearly identifiable is 'history from below': the attempt to recapture the experiences, attitudes, value-systems and perspectives of those left out of traditional history (and most published primary sources). After all, one would expect Marxist historians to show an interest in those classes whose exploitation had left so few records. We can see their interest in so-called grass-roots history, in Thompson's *Making of the English Working Class* and in Hill's T*he World Turned Upside Down*. Hill, for example, deliberately takes what he calls 'the worm's eye view' as he looks at radical ideas during the period of Oliver Cromwell. However, Hobsbawm admits to some limitations to the Marxist contribution to 'history from below'. He accepts that Marxists - or, in fact, socialist historians in general - were tempted to study ordinary people as and when they could be seen as contributors to the forward march of the labour movement. This led to a concentration on institutions and organisations which represented the workers, rather than the workers themselves. Similarly, George Rudé's attempt to recover the mentalities of the crowd is less a desire to explore the world-view and feelings of ordinary people than to examine the attitudes of those people in potentially revolutionary situations.

There are other limitations to the influence of Marxism. Peter Burke is full of praise for the two books by Hill and Thompson cited above, but he has one major worry which echoes the point just made: that the 'ordinary people' chosen are there because they were suitably exploited, or suitably radical. Thompson, he argues, comes close to excluding the very real phenomenon of the working-class Tory; Hill tends to forget that not all radicals were ordinary people, and that not all ordinary people were radicals. Burke comments that, to Thompson and Hill, 'some people are considered as more people than others.'[7] We might add that Hill is understandably fascinated by the ideas of early communists like the Diggers or the remarkably subversive, blaspheming and outrageous Ranters. But this is not really 'people's history' or 'history from below' in the sense of recapturing the experiences of ordinary people. Particularly in the case of Hill, we see an historian out to recapture those who were excluded from traditional histories because he finds their ideas stimulating and - crucially - of use to us today. They are recaptured on his terms, and his net is not spread for those who had less interesting things to say. However, one should accept that the Marxist historians have done much to recover the thoughts and actions of radical groups languishing in undeserved obscurity.

The relationship between Marxism and women's history is somewhat problematic. As we have seen, Marxism certainly played a part in the attack on élitist (and male-dominated) political and diplomatic history, and so helped to open the door to a much wider definition of what constituted the discipline of history. Practitioners of Marxist and feminist history wish to make their contribution to political and social change. Both Marxism and women's history share an awareness of exploitation, but also frequently wish to point to achievement: in other words, to demonstrate the extent to which those discriminated against were able, against all the odds, to make their own histories. However, women's history is offering an alternative way of structuring the past to that offered by class analysis and economic determinism. In one form, it seeks to recapture the experience of women and so offer 'her-story' as opposed to 'his-story'. On the other hand, in the form of gender history, it seeks to explore how the power structures in society are based on gender rather than on class. Marxism has little part to play in such analyses.

How can we summarize the contemporary value of Marxism to historiography? Marxist history has certainly been both shaken and stirred by politics, economics, philosophy and, not least, by the writing of history itself. Its status as a scientific exposition of laws of history, taught in its crudest form in communist countries, has not really survived the near-collapse of communism as a political and economic power in Europe and beyond. A theory which rests upon a particular line of progress which projects into the future is clearly vulnerable when the future turns out to be an unanticipated one. The political breakdown of communism and the apparent triumphs of capitalism encouraged a deep suspicion of any form of wide-ranging and theoretical explanations (sometimes termed a *metanarrative*) which can express itself as postmodernism (see Chapter 5) or, for practising historians, in the desire to play down the very concept of revolution. J.C.D. Clark's book on state and society in seventeenth and eighteenth-century England is significantly titled *Revolution and Rebellion*. Clark comments: 'Rebellion rather than revolution is thus the crucial explanatory category for revisionist historians.'[8] He refers to Hill, Thompson, Rudé and Hobsbawm as the 'Marxist Old Guard': a not-very-subtle ploy to suggest that their day - along with Marxists in general - has gone. But has it? I think not. Had the British Marxists written in the manner of East German or Soviet Party-men, then we would be waving them goodbye. But their blend of a sophisticated use of class-struggle analysis, their refusal to offer crude simplifications of the base-superstructure model, their willingness to subscribe to the need to provide evidence for their contentions, their frequent mastery of an astonishing range of sources - all these suggest that their influence is likely to remain and that Marxist history is anything but dead. Were it so, then Clark and others who share his views would have no need to write as revisionists. In general, Marxist history is a great stimulus to historians of every type to consider some of the most fundamental ideas. What is the place of theory in the writing of history? How far are men and women free agents or the product of impersonal forces? Is there a pattern to history? Are we to reject the thought that the writing of history serves a political purpose? Of course, it is easy enough to say that Marxists (or any other historians who employ a model to structure their analysis) select evidence which fits the model and ignore evidence which conflicts with or seems inappropriate to it. And we have expressed concern about what is meant by the economic base ultimately creating the superstructure. Distortions will and do occur for these reasons. But we have already seen that distortion occurs in many ways in the writing of history: in the selection of a particular type of source, or the omission of another; in claiming not only objectivity, but also neutrality as well. Distortion is not a characteristic of Marxist historiography alone.

5 The Emergence of the *Annales* School and 'Total History'

The massive economic, political and social changes of the nineteenth century were, as we have seen, instrumental in generating distinctive types of history. The legacy of Ranke could be applied to the history of nation-states and, if sufficiently distorted, serve the needs of self-confident new nations like Germany. The growth of Marxist history and economic history similarly reflected those changes. In Britain, the belief in the superiority of British institutions and the British way of liberal parliamentary democracy stimulated the kind of history (known pejoratively as 'Whig history') which traced the development of British 'freedoms' through time and, inevitably, encouraged the historian to judge individuals in history by their supposed contribution - or otherwise - to the progress of liberalism (see pages 66-70).

The dreadful carnage of the First World War and the subsequent economic depressions led a number of historians to question history which fed the needs of the nation-states that had started the wars in the first place. For some, this of course led to the adopting of Marxism; for others, it led to an increasing dissatisfaction with traditional 'event-centred' history and a desire to widen the scope of history both in terms of methodology and in subject-matter. In France, even before the First World War, there was a movement against what was seen as German obsession with the grubbing up of facts and/or theories of development and dominance (sometimes in defence of the kind of expansionism which had led to the seizing of Alsace and Lorraine from France in 1871). In some cases, French historians became interested in interdisciplinary approaches - using, say, human geography or the relatively new discipline of sociology. An interdisciplinary approach does not fit very well with a history dominated by the narration of 'great events', often performed by 'great men'. It would suit an approach focusing on deep-seated economic, social or political structures underpinning events and on problems rather than description.

These, in fact, are essential characteristics of the so-called *Annales* historians. The name comes from the journal, *Annales d'histoire économique et sociale*, founded by the medievalist Marc Bloch and the sixteenth-century specialist Lucien Febvre in 1929. Peter Burke[9] identifies a first phase of the movement in the period from the 1920s to 1945, where we see a radically subversive attack on traditional French political narrative history.

6 Marc Bloch (1886-1944)

Marc Bloch operated on the basis that history meant the study of the past, not the study of documents. This is not to deny his expertise in documentary analysis, but to recognise that he saw such inquiries as only one aspect of an historian's work. An early (1913) study of the area around Paris, the Île-de-France, emphasized the importance of geography. Specifically, Bloch used a study of landscape and townscape to help establish the characteristics of the region. Already, Bloch was approaching history by setting himself a question to answer, rather than simply taking an accepted historical period and describing the doings of the élites therein. Bloch certainly liked his questions to be broad ones. In 1924, whilst a professor at the University of Strasburg, he wrote *Les rois thaumaturges* (English title, T*he Royal Touch*; literally, *Miracle-working Kings*), which asked the question 'How could people believe in the illusion that kings had a healing touch?'. This book displayed his interest in group psychology (or more specifically 'collective mentalities') and a willingness to show how those mentalities interconnected with political institutions. He did not restrict himself to France, but tackled the way in which kingship was also given a supernatural character in England. In 1931, his short book *French Rural History* explored the links between landscape, rural customs, and political and social institutions. He divided

France into three regions based on the differences in terrain, soil and climate and argued that rural life was the product of these and other inter-related factors (including religion, mentalities, royal policies and monetary developments) over an impressive time-scale (early medieval to the French Revolution). Class was by no means ignored, but was not seen as a shaper in the Marxist sense. Bloch, in fact, had no time for historians who wrote with a predetermined thesis in mind, and was more than prepared to admit that his own conclusions were often tentative. The range of evidence used was inevitably very broad, and included archaeology, place names and modern estate maps. Bloch's *Feudal Society* (1939-40) also tackled the study of society through time, covering the period 900-1300AD throughout Europe (and beyond). It is vital to understand that Bloch was not writing the standard type of institutional or legalistic history of feudalism, but rather a work which explored social structure through a very wide range of skills: in language, literature, group psychology, geography, economics and, of course, the critical evaluation of a variety of sources both documentary and visual. At the heart of *Feudal Society* was Bloch's examination of feudal culture through a discussion of modes of thought, feeling and attitude: in short, mentalities. For example, Bloch explored the medieval concept of time: an obvious interest for an historian who spoke of history as the 'science of men in time'. Carole Fink[10], an understandably enthusiastic biographer of Bloch, accepts the shortcomings of the work, including the way in which it fails to discuss the roles of the middle class and clergy. One might add that Bloch's handling of the political background was sketchy, and that his attempt to locate modern nationalism in a feudal past was less than convincing. Nevertheless, as a wide-ranging and innovative analysis of the development of social relationships, it has great merit to this day.

Equally appealing, perhaps, is the way in which Bloch's vision of history - with its demands for probing questions and an unfettered spirit of enquiry - interwove with his commitment to the liberal values of twentieth-century France. As a Jewish teenager, he had seen the defeat of the army and anti-Semitic elements in French society in the infamous Dreyfus case, where a Jewish army officer had been accused and found guilty (on forged evidence) of passing military information to Germany. Dreyfus was exonerated by the courts in 1906, and it is not too fanciful to see Bloch's insistence on critical method, the interrogation of evidence and a delight in exposing forgeries as a reflection of his interest in and regard for the processes of law. His commitment to France was absolute. He fought in both World Wars, joined and became a leader of the Resistance (code-name 'Narbonne'), was captured, tortured and shot.

7 Lucien Febvre (1878-1956)

One man who embarked on the sad search for the missing Bloch in 1944 was his colleague Lucien Febvre. Febvre's career ran parallel to Bloch's when they both taught at the University of Strasbourg, but his rise through the ranks of the French historical profession was significantly smoother and faster (in part because, as a non-Jew, he was not faced with the anti-Semitism which obstructed Bloch all too often). In 1933, he was appointed one of the professors in the highly prestigious research institution, the Collège de France. Despite all his efforts, Bloch was never able to follow him there. Febvre interpreted his success in getting a chair at the Collège de France as an endorsement of the approach championed by Bloch and himself through the founding of the *Annales* journal. It was no such thing, but Febvre was a first-rate propagandist and advocate in the corridors of French scholarship and used his combative personality and skills to ensure that the *Annales* approach became the single most dominant force in French historiography. After the end of the Second World War, he was made president of the so-called Sixth (social sciences) Section of the *Ecole Pratique des Hautes Etudes.* This was the ideal base from which to shape the French historical establishment.

What, then, were Febvre's aims? He stuck firmly to the manifesto of the very first *Annales* issue: namely, the emphasis on the need for interdisciplinary work, the adopting of a problem-solving approach and a desire to move beyond political narrative. His early work reflected a particular interest in geography. His *Philippe II et la France-Comté* (1912) opened with a geographical outline of this region of France, and he followed it up with a work on historical geography in general, *La terre et l'évolution humaine* (1922). Subsequent work on Reformation history concerned itself with religious attitudes rather than focusing, in the traditional manner, on the churches as institutions. The very title of his book *The Problem of Unbelief in the Sixteenth Century: the religion of Rabelais* (1942) reflects the way in which he both structured his work around an explicit problem and also concentrated on collective mentalities (though Febvre preferred the phrase 'mental apparatus' or *'outillage mental'*). The impact of Febvre's own writings was restricted to France in the main, but he bequeathed the *Annales* approach to his co-worker Fernand Braudel.

8 Fernand Braudel (1902-85)

Braudel taught in schools in the French colony of Algeria and then in Paris before taking up a post at the University of São Paulo in Brazil (1935-8). His experience in Brazil gave him a less eurocentric perspective than most of his contemporaries. He spent the war years in a German prison camp, writing his doctoral thesis. This was an astonishing achievement which, in the absence of books, stretched his prodigious memory to the limit. The thesis emerged in 1949 as possibly his greatest and certainly his most influential book: *The Mediterranean and the Mediterranean World in the Age of Philip II*. To Febvre, he owed its central focus - the sea itself. It was originally envisaged as a study of Philip II's foreign policy, but Febvre encouraged him in his distaste for traditional accounts of the sixteenth century through battles and 'great leaders'. In the preface to the first edition, and speaking of previous studies dealing with the Mediterranean area, Braudel said:

1 So many of these studies speak a language of the past, outdated in more
   ways than one. Their concern is not the sea in all its complexity, but
   some minute piece of the mosaic, not the grand movement of
   Mediterranean life, but the actions of a few princes and rich men, the
5 trivia of the past, bearing little relation to the slow and powerful march
   of history which is our subject.

Instead, this huge book (six times the size of the standard volume) was divided into three parts, each with a different use of the concept of time and each with a different approach to the subject-matter of history. The first part was what Braudel called 'geo-history', and concentrated on the way in which geographical features underpin all other history. The relationship between the environment and humankind is intimate, but inevitably change is virtually undetectable: 'almost timeless', as Braudel put it. Mountains, for instance, shape cultures and attitudes. They isolate, create psychological and social barriers between those who live there and those who live in the more productive valleys. The second part ('Collective destinies and general trends') concerned the history of:

the slow but perceptible rhythms ... studying in turn economic systems,
states, societies, civilizations and finally, in order to convey more clearly
my conception of history, attempting to show how all these deep-seated
forces were at work in the complex arena of warfare.

What we have here is the history of the structures without which the actions of people make little sense: communication systems, supply of raw materials and currency. The third and final part 'gives a hearing', as Braudel put it, to traditional history: namely, the fast-moving but superficial history of events and individuals.

1 ... what Paul Lacombe and François Simiand call *l'histoire événémentielle*,
   that is, the history of events: surface disturbances, crests of foam that
   the tides of history carry on their strong backs ... Resounding events
   are often only momentary outbursts, surface manifestations of these
5 larger movements and explicable only in terms of them.

The Mediterranean stunned Braudel's fellow historians in France, and one can see why. He demanded that the historian should consider time in a different way - or rather in different ways, because time is not uniform. There is geographical time, as in Part one, social time, as in Part two, and individual time, as in Part three. But it is clear where Braudel attached the greatest importance: to *la longue durée*, or the slow, long-term changes of geographical and social time. History of this type must cross disciplinary boundaries in the same way as its sheer scale should ignore borders between countries and time-scales based on the brief reigns of individuals like kings. The aim here is for a 'total history', which we might define as the attempt to integrate all aspects of past human life - cultural, social, economic, political. It is the quest for total history which was to be perhaps the most significant characteristic of those working within or alongside the *Annales* school as led by Braudel. 'Total history' was certainly a term used by Braudel (as was 'Global history'), but it is important to be aware that he meant it as an approach - almost an attitude of mind - whereby one tries to extend the boundaries of problems as far as possible rather than a literal attempt to write the history of the totality of the human past.

Given the scope of *The Mediterranean* and the breathtaking ambition of Braudel's undertaking, it is hardly surprising that the book is open to criticism. Despite the influence of Bloch and Febvre, Braudel showed little interest in collective mentalities, even though belief and value-systems must have played a significant role in an area which witnessed the confrontation between Christianity and Islam. Secondly, the third part of the book is not integrated with the other parts and perhaps reflects Braudel's relative lack of interest in events and past politics. Traditional historians certainly objected to the downgrading of politics, but Braudel was at the very least forcing them - and all historians - to justify the writing of history dominated by politics. However, it is certainly open to question whether, in downplaying the significance of individuals and political life, Braudel failed to appreciate the very real impact people can have on structures. *The Mediterranean* appears to be highly determinist, leaving little freedom for human responsibility and action. Also, the work is open to the criticism (often made by Marxists) that Braudel (and the *Annales* school as a whole) failed to explain why and how change in structures actually took place.

Taken all in all, few historians had the expertise to emulate the astonishing range of a book like *The Mediterranean*. The subsequent development of *Annales* historiography in France reflected the difficulties inherent in trying to write a global or total history on such a scale. The period of Braudel's ascendancy as president of the Sixth Section and director of the *Annales* journal was marked by the emerging of two main strands in *Annales* history: a growing emphasis on history based on statistical data - quantitative history - and the attempt to write total history of a relatively narrow area. These approaches are by no means mutually exclusive.

The growth of quantitative history within *Annales* owed more to an historian on the fringes of the movement, the Marxist Ernest Labrousse, than it did to Braudel, Bloch or Febvre. It is interesting to speculate, as Burke does, that the greater emphasis on quantitative history in the second edition of *The Mediterranean* reflected the influence of Labrousse on Braudel himself. Quantitative history complements well the emphasis on trends of the *longue durée*. It is significant that the work of one of Braudel's research students, Pierre Chaunu, should attempt to combine the massive thesis based on a huge area (in his case, the Atlantic in *Seville and the Atlantic*) with a concentration on quantitative history (in the form of economic trends). It is largely through the work of Chaunu that two words became a part of the *Annales* vocabulary and mind-set: *conjoncture* for the medium or shorter term and *structure* for the longer term. This is not to say that Chaunu ignored mentalities in his focus on quantitative history. He has led a research team investigating the changing attitudes to death, but through a detailed examination of thousands of wills rather than through the literary sources which provide a less statistical insight into value-systems.

Since, as we have suggested, few historians could match the mind-boggling length of *The Mediterranean* and *Seville and the Atlantic*, there developed the tendency for followers to write more restricted regional histories, focusing on a town or a well-defined province - often split into sections tackling *structure* and *conjoncture*.

9 Emmanuel Le Roy Ladurie (b.1929)

In the early work of Le Roy Ladurie, we can trace with ease the influence of both Labrousse and Braudel. His doctoral thesis, published as *The Peasants of Languedoc* (1966), was predictably huge, had a Braudel-style introduction in the geo-historical manner and settled into a detailed discussion of fluctuations in prices, birth rates and so on in the manner of Labrousse. However, it avoided the *structure/conjoncture* framework in favour of a more chronological approach and, significantly, looked at the impact of the economy from the perspective of ordinary people. In short, Le Roy Ladurie was starting to bring people into *Annales* history in a way which was foreign to his predecessors. This vital development was made concrete in his book *Montaillou* (1975) which became a best-seller among general readers. Montaillou is a village in south-west France - an area which, in the fourteenth century, was heavily influenced by the heresy of the Cathars. The Cathars represented the most fundamental of challenges to the Catholic Church and to Christian belief. They denied the validity of the priesthood of the Catholic church and its sacraments and also the Incarnation of Christ. Suspected Cathars in the Montaillou area were identified and examined by the local bishop, and the record of interrogations has survived (published in 1965). Twenty-five inhabitants of Montaillou were interrogated, and Le Roy

Ladurie used the techniques of anthropology to help recreate the world of the villagers from these records. Chapter headings reveal his approach. In Part one, *The Ecology of Montaillou*, he discussed such issues as the mental outlook of the shepherds. The table of contents for Part two is shown below.

Montaillou is more than a study of mentalities, because he allowed the people of the village to speak, and used their words to reconstruct their world. A straightforward example would be his use of the words of the villager Alazaïs Azéma:

> 1 *Eighteen years ago … when I had just brought my pigs out of my house, I met Raymond Belot leaning on his stick in the square in front of the château. He said to me:-'Come into my house'. I answered:'No - I have left my door open.'* This passage suggests that people and pigs lived together
> 5 in the same house …

Jim Sharpe,[11] writing on 'history from below', sees *Montaillou* as a landmark in that, like oral history, it allows the historian to get close to people's actual words. The point is taken, and no-one would deny that it is a wonderfully vivid book. But *Montaillou* is nonetheless open to major criticisms. The first is that Le Roy Ladurie treated his source in a curiously uncritical way. Why should an inquisitor's report be taken as an unbiased record of the villagers' words? And where is the attempt at generalisation that one usually expects from the historian? Of what, might we ask, is the village of Montaillou typical?

10 The Different Strands within the *Annales* School

It would seem that, as the *Annales*-type history conquered the French historical establishment in the years of Braudel's ascendancy, its various strands developed lives of their own. Quantitative history remained an important element, and the Febvre-style stress on mentalities was extended into discussions of the history of the body, dreams, smells. To investigate this kind of history demands the multi-disciplinary approach which, of course, lay at the heart of the ambitions of Bloch and Febvre. In an illuminating paper on the 'history of the body', Roy Porter[12] recognises the great contribution in that field played by *Annaliste* scholarship through its demands for a total history, and also points to the need for historians of the body to exploit the insights afforded by such disciplines as cultural anthropology and sociology. And then, of course, we have the micro-history of the town or village in an attempt to make total history manageable.

However, there remains the issue of events. Reluctantly or otherwise, some *Annales* historians have displayed an increasing awareness that events cannot be ignored. In part this could be seen as a reaction against the determinism of Marxists and that of the later Braudel. Le Roy Ladurie has spoken of the 'creative event' which stimulates the transition from one structure to another, and wrote a book which had an event as its focus: *Carnival: A People's Uprising at Romans 1579-1580* (1979). The traditional Mardi Gras carnival had turned into a bloody conflict, and Le Roy Ladurie commented that, to gauge its importance, one must keep in mind the fact that it happened

> at the juncture of two essential phases of the Wars of Religion, a bitter struggle between Protestants and Catholics involving France and much of the Western world during the second half of the sixteenth century.

He later added:

> Although it was a strictly localized incident, the Carnival in Romans represents a deep probe into the geological stratifications of a dated culture.

So Le Roy Ladurie was not leaving structures behind. He saw the carnival as an illustration of these long-term trends and social and economic systems that make up the structures of history.

11 The Impact of the *Annales* Historians

On France, the impact of *Annales*-style history in the time of Braudel is undeniable. It took over the historical establishment. Its impact elsewhere has been variable. Peter Burke, in *The French Historical Revolution*, offers a convenient summary. He argues that there was little impact in Britain before the 1970s, when translations of works by *Annales* historians started to become available in numbers. The reasons are not hard to find. Fundamental words like *structure* and *conjoncture* do not translate readily, and the barrage of quantitative detail which frequently accompanied them had no real echo in the approaches of the vast majority of British historians. The British

Marxists were more sympathetic and much more interested, but not particularly keen on borrowing directly from *Annales*. Eric Hobsbawm speaks of the respect felt by those who founded the left-wing journal *Past and Present* for their illustrious French colleagues - but it was a respect founded on the shared dislike for 'establishment' history rather than a desire to imitate. Nor does Hobsbawm think that those interested in mentalities in Britain owed that interest to *Annales*, but to what he calls a home-grown interest in culture in a 'quasi-anthropological sense'[13]. Neither have Germany or North America proved to be fertile ground for *Annales*. The more personal links forged by Polish historians studying in Paris and the legacy of Braudel from his work in South America have been more productive.

Even so, *Annales* history deserves to be recognized for what it is: a challenging, stimulating alternative to traditional political and diplomatic history and to the model-based history of Marxists. Braudel points out eloquently that *Annales'* service was to 'plead in favour of a community of the human sciences, despite the walls that separate them from one another.' Perhaps we should leave the last words with Peter Burke, who sees *Annales* historians as perhaps the single most important source of inspiration for the 'New History' which has come to represent the breaking down of the restrictive, Rankean-style model of the true concerns of the historian - politics, and yet more politics. Everything and everyone has a history, and *Annales* did much to make that clear.

12 Conclusion

The last two chapters have taken us through over two hundred years of the writing of history. We have witnessed the development of the professional historian and a curious, almost dialectical pattern in historiography. The period of the Enlightenment was marked by the frequent attempt to use the past as evidence of the workings of laws of human behaviour. Such history was often judgemental and lacked a full methodology, but it was wide-ranging and not restricted to political history. In reaction to it, we saw the development of the Rankean method and approach whose legacy was a narrowing of history to the political and diplomatic behaviour of the élites. The intensive study of records and the PhD were born: the pursuit of history required the detached and objective scholar who was writing history for its own sake. But alongside this immensely influential Rankean approach grew up its near antithesis, the wide-ranging theories of Marxism. And there were other alternatives to Ranke, including the growth of the multi-disciplinary *Annales* School and its call for total history. History is no longer just past politics, but past everything. And now, even within *Annales*, there are signs of a recognition that narrative, event-centred history cannot and should not be ignored. If this is confusion, at least it is healthy confusion. Historians are forced to think about the nature of their subject, and this is a good thing.

References
1 Peter Singer, *Marx* (Oxford University Press, 1980), p.38.
2 Eric Hobsbawm, 'The Historians' Group of the Communist Party' in Maurice Cornforth (ed.), *Rebels and their Causes. Essays in honour of A.L. Morton* (Lawrence & Wishart, 1978), p.22.
3 Ibid., p.26.
4 Ibid., p.38.
5 Harvey J. Kaye, *The British Marxist Historians* (Polity, 1984), see pp.99-130.
6 R.W. Fogel and G.R. Elton, *Which Road to the Past? Two Views of History* (Yale University Press,1983), p.29.
7 Peter Burke, 'People's history or total history' in Raphael Samuel (ed.), *People's History and Socialist Theory* (Routledge & Kegan Paul, 1981), p.7.
8 J.C.D. Clark, *Revolution and Rebellion: State and society in England in the seventeenth and eighteenth centuries* (Cambridge University Press, 1986), p.23.
9 Peter Burke, *The French Historical Revolution: The Annales School, 1929-89* (Polity, 1990).
10 Carole Fink, *Marc Bloch: A Life in History* (Cambridge University Press, 1991).
11 Jim Sharpe, 'History from Below' in Peter Burke (ed.), *New Perspectives on Historical Writing* (Polity, 1991), pp.24-31.
12 Roy Porter, 'History of the Body', in Burke, ibid., pp.206-32.
13 Eric Hobsbawm, *On History* (Weidenfeld & Nicolson, 1997), p.183

Making notes on 'From Karl Marx and Marxism to the Annales School'

I recommend once again the 'large diagram' style of making notes for this chapter, but the standard criteria which make up the headings of the diagram should be adapted to meet the needs of likely examination questions. Marx is not primarily an historian, and it therefore makes no sense to try to use Marx himself in an essay demanding an analysis of an historian's qualities. Note-making should therefore focus on the IMPACT of Marxist historiography. It is important that you link your understanding of Marx's ideas with a discussion of his impact. The diagram on the next page should encourage this.

Summary Diagrams
Marx and Marxist Historiography

Definition of economic determinism

The debate over how determinist Marx was

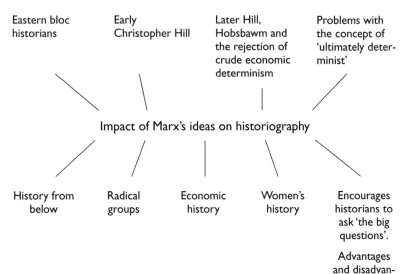

Eastern bloc historians

Early Christopher Hill

Later Hill, Hobsbawm and the rejection of crude economic determinism

Problems with the concept of 'ultimately deter- minist'

Impact of Marx's ideas on historiography

History from below

Radical groups

Economic history

Women's history

Encourages historians to ask 'the big questions'.

Advantages and disadvan- tages of the model-based approach

The Annales *School*

Annales - A problem-based, interdisciplinary approach to history, focusing on structures of society rather than events and on the search for 'Total History'

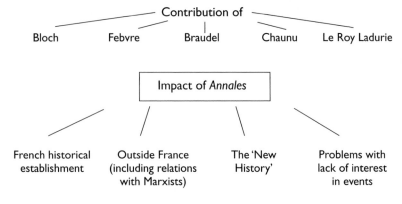

Contribution of

Bloch   Febvre   Braudel   Chaunu   Le Roy Ladurie

Impact of *Annales*

French historical establishment

Outside France (including relations with Marxists)

The 'New History'

Problems with lack of interest in events

Answering essay questions on 'From Karl Marx and Marxism to the Annales School'

Remember that you must not attempt to answer questions on the qualities of the historian by using Marx as an example. His importance - from our perspective - lies in his contribution to historiography.

You might make use of his theories in essays which focus on types of explanation. For example, you might be asked to write a critical evaluation of any theory (or theories) which explain the past by means of models, patterns or theories of progress. The obvious plan for this type of essay would be based around advantages and disadvantages. Use this approach in constructing a plan to answer one of the following questions:

1. To what extent does the writing of history benefit from the use of models based on a theory of progress?
2. How far should one attempt to identify patterns in the past?

You will need, of course, to root your discussion of disadvantages in the alternative offered by the Rankean tradition. But any answer to these questions would also benefit from specific examples chosen from whatever period of history you have studied in some detail.

The *Annales* school lends itself to several types of question. You might be asked to comment on the way in which other subjects complement the study of history, and could certainly use the *Annales* historians as a focus for such an essay:

3. Discuss the academic subjects which, alongside history, would be of most benefit to the study of history.
4. How far should history be a subject studied purely by historians?

These questions do, of course, demand a coverage of the relationship between history and, say, psychology or anthropology, which is outside the scope of this book. On psychology, however, you might find the comments on Namier (pages 72-74) of help.

The *Annales* school would be an ideal example to use when answering a wide-ranging question such as:

5. How far should historians restrict themselves to the study of events?

And, inevitably, there are the 'contribution to historiography' questions. Advice on tackling these is given on page 79.

6. Discuss the contribution to the development of historical study of Fernand Braudel.

Rather trickier might be:

7. What qualities make an historian worthy of study? Illustrate your answer by reference to the work of at least two historians.

The key phrase is, of course, 'worthy of study'. You would be well advised to define this in your introduction. You might feel that an historian would be worthy of study if he had made a significant contribution to the development of a scholarly technique, to widening the scope of history and/or had inspired other historians to follow him (and so had founded a 'school' of history).

1. Marxist Historiography

Read the extracts from Christopher Hill's *The English Revolution 1640* (page 89) and *A Turbulent, Seditious and Factious People* (page 90) and answer the following questions.

a) What evidence is there that Hill is adopting economic determinism in a 'crude' form? (5 marks)

b) How far does the extract from Hill's work on Bunyan (page 90) reflect a rejection of economic determinism? (5 marks)

2. Braudel, time and events

Read the extracts from *The Mediterranean* on page 99 and answer the following questions.

a) Explain Braudel's attitudes to event-centred history. (5 marks).

b) What criticisms might be made of Braudel's views on the subject-matter of history? (5 marks)

3. Le Roy Ladurie and Montaillou

Read the extracts on page 102 and answer the following questions.

a) What characteristics of Le Roy Ladurie as an historian are revealed by the extracts from *Montaillou*? (6 marks)

b) What criticisms might be made of Le Roy Ladurie's use of original sources? (4 marks)

5 Defining History

1 The Noise of Battle

A definition of history? One might think that this chapter ought to be uncontroversial, and maybe even a total waste of time. Perhaps so: in which case let me offer, tongue in cheek, a straightforward definition. *History is the past, and historians are those who study and write about history.* At first sight, this seems reasonable, if a little dull. But this apparently simple definition leads us straight into a bitterly-contested war zone, torn by the violent disagreements of those who write about history. For the wary as well as the unwary, it is a mine-field. Some of the combatants have advice for us. There is no point, they say, in trying to get off the battlefield or to flee the war. Conflict is part of the human condition: we should embrace it, enjoy it, pick up weapons to suit us and blaze away ourselves. There will never be peace.

You might think that I have overdone the military metaphor. Surely historians can conduct a reasonably good-tempered debate on a subject which, after all, ought to have been sorted out long ago? In fact, the debate is a very real one, accompanied by some rather violent and unscholarly language as historians see their cherished assumptions subjected to destructive irony. Nor is the military metaphor a product of my fevered imagination. A recent book by Richard Evans is entitled *In Defence of History,* and the blurb on the dust-jacket talks of the 'disintegrative attack' to which the writing of history has been exposed.

What, then, are the issues which generate such imagery? We can start with my simple and apparently incontrovertible definition of history and identify some of the problems with it.

i)   It is all very well saying that history is the past, but, in practice, is it not the actual writing about the past by historians, rather than the past itself? After all, the words of historians are virtually all we have. Granted, there are traces of the past all around us, in buildings, landscape, memories and documents. But when we try to explain, to give some structure to the past, then our words do not actually let the past live. We impose ourselves on it. No historian can recreate the past. If she or he could, then our lives would be very strange and frightening.

ii)   So, one could argue that there is no such thing as history in the sense of 'the past' at all. All we have is what we write about it. Taking this a stage further, it has been argued that when we study history what we are actually studying is historiography: the past as seen in the words of historians.

iii) So, we then end up with the problem of the historians and what they do to the past. This means that the past is in the hands of people who are going to shape it to reflect their own political, social, cultural, religious and educational stances. In other words, the past is never handed on to us directly. There can never be real objectivity.

iv) Yes, but what about the original sources themselves - the primary evidence or traces, as they are often called? Might we not let them speak to us, and thereby get the real thing with an absolute minimum of interference from our increasingly-discredited historian?

v) Fine, but there are a number of problems here. Firstly, such sources are themselves compromised by the distortions of the original writers - distortions which we cannot always detect. In any case, one cannot simply lump together a group of sources on, say, England under William the Conqueror and pronounce, 'Right! This is what it was like.' Sources are not designed with the needs of future generations in mind. There will be massive gaps - in the case of eleventh-century England, there will be almost nothing about the majority of the population. And then, of course, along comes the historian to make a selection to suit himself. In any case, if the writing of history involves some sort of explanation, then this is where the historian comes in. He is our guide, and gives us the context into which these sources fit. He sifts, analyses, makes something coherent out of traces which are not in themselves coherent. What we get is the historian's view of eleventh-century England, even if he has given us little more than a set of sources with a linking text. What we do not get is eleventh-century England.

vi) There is a final argument. Briefly, it is not so much that we cannot possibly detect the truth about the past - although, of course, we cannot. It is more that we cannot detect truth anyway. To believe that humankind can do so is merely to deceive oneself. It is therefore best to see history as a set of texts on the subject of the past which are, in essence, fictional. The historian is therefore a type of literary scholar who takes a text to pieces to show how it works rather than being somebody who reflects reality in any way.

vii) On the other hand, one could see most of the above points as unhelpful philosophical posturing which denies the common sense view that historians do use the traces of the past to create a picture which is close to, but never the ultimate, truth.

As I said, a battlefield. The reader might hope to get a guide to the campaign, a way of avoiding it altogether or at least some decent weapons with which to enter the conflict. At the very least, we should be able to alight on a workable definition of history. Perhaps! At least, you should be in a position to make up your own mind by the end of the chapter.

2 Postmodernism

To squeeze the last drops out of my military metaphor, this important section should be seen as the biting of the bullet. Postmodernism is perhaps the most radical and significant challenge to the 'common sense' view of what the historian does. It is also a challenge to those who set out to write genuinely introductory books on history. This is partly because there is no such thing as a postmodern school of historians with a convenient and single approach which one can describe in a straightforward way. It is partly because postmodernism is interdisciplinary and feeds upon ideas from such fields as linguistics and anthropology in which the historian rarely has expertise. However, the main problem is easily stated: postmodernist theory is difficult to understand. To be frank, some of the major theorists enjoy being provocative, ironical and - it has to be said - obscure. Depending on your viewpoint, this sort of thing can be stimulating. But it is not easy to follow. So, I propose to tackle this by adopting an approach which some might find hard to swallow. Section 3 will offer a briefish summary of postmodernist views on history. This will, of course, lay me open to the charge of simplification and over-generalisation. I might also be accused of setting up my own target at which to aim. Subsequent sections will - hopefully - allow me to repair some of the damage by giving me the chance to expand upon and discuss the issues raised in section 3.

3 Postmodernism and History: an Introduction

Let us start with what the word 'postmodern' actually means. The term was first applied to particular approaches in the creative arts in the 1970s. As the word suggests, it involves a deliberate rejection of 'modernism'. Postmodern architects, for example, poked fun at the systematic, regular, rational, 'style-fits-use' buildings constructed by their modernist colleagues. Postmodernist buildings were whimsical, ironic, irregular (see page 113). In philosophy, postmodernism also represents an attack on so-called modernist thinking. Modernism was seen as a set of assumptions which held that it was possible for the fundamentally rational humankind to discover systematically certain scientific laws about the way the world operated. Such discoveries would allegedly lead to progress.

Postmodernism questions the validity of modernist theories, on the grounds that they are simply the product of a mistaken belief (characteristic of modernism) in what human reason is and can do. We may think we are objective, rational, able to look at our world, describe what it actually is, analyse what makes it tick and suggest ways of making it tick better and faster. But this is a delusion for two main reasons. Firstly, what we claim as objective knowledge about society is very often just a way of getting power over other people. We decide what makes 'true' knowledge and then control access to it. This can range from denying a particular type of education to women to assuming that Western democracy is more civilised than any other form of political life and that non-Western societies need help (or control) to be 'civilised'.

In any case, ask postmodernists, can we really see ourselves as rational, scientific and objective when those supposed guardians of our civilisation, the scientific community, encouraged the development of weapons of mass destruction? Where has technological advance led us? To the pollution of our planet and even greater inequality of wealth throughout the world? To the postmodernist, all the old certainties about progress or even religious belief have been exploded. We are the better for their departure. It is liberating to realise that 'truth' may be out of our reach.

There is a further reason for arguing that our belief in the all-conquering power of human reason is a delusion. Quite simply, we are all prisoners of language. We can know most things only indirectly, and only through words. This is particularly true for history, of course, because we can have no direct experience of the past. Being so dependent on words would not matter so much if we were in control of the words used by others or even by ourselves. But we are not. If we settle down to write, say, an accurate, calm, factual and objective account of some event in history, then what we produce can never be the truth about the past. We have been using documents - texts - from the past. We have been using the texts of other historians. And now we have produced our own text. But each text, including our own, is anything but an objective and factual account. Texts, whether we like it or not, are full of metaphors, symbols, signs, gaps, deliberate and accidental omissions and distortions. And where do these come from? They reflect the power-relationships of the given society, the conscious and unconscious attitudes of the author towards those relationships; the position of the author within that society - and a host of distortions both personal and public which cannot be allowed for in any typical and superficial analysis of 'bias'. If we take these texts to bits - subject them to a process of deconstructive literary analysis - we can hope to identify some of these symbols, gaps and distortions. But we are going to use words ourselves in writing up our conclusions, and so are going to be the prisoners of language in the same way. The most honest approach in writing history is to accept that the closest our work will get to the 'truth' is to put across our own version of what the 'truth' is. If this is useful to us and to people who share our particular set of ideals or prejudices, all well and good. In fact, there is really no such thing as 'history', just 'historiography'. We must never forget that historians who claim to be writing about the

An example of postmodernist architecture

past as it actually happened are almost laughably naïve. In any case, their belief that the truth is there to be found in an objective and 'scientific' sense is the kind of modernist illusion we need to do away with in the postmodernist era. The history we write is really fiction. Let us be honest, at least.

So far, I have suggested that defining history is massively controversial. I have also suggested that postmodernism currently represents the most far-reaching and radical attempt to define history, and one which short-circuits traditional definitions. We now need to clothe the skeleton by expanding on the summary.

4 The Origins of Postmodernism

a) Modernism

Since, as we have seen, Postmodernism exists in opposition to so-called 'modernism', we should look at the charges made against modernism. Remember, though, that there is no obligation on us to accept that 'modernism' is a meaningful term in practice.

Modernism, we recall, is supposedly a world-view which assumes that human reason can detect reality or truth, and that we are capable of judging ideas by comparing them to that reality. There is, of course, nothing self-evident about this. One could equally argue that human reason is weak: that human beings are too violent, too emotional, to be able to recognise truth even if it walked up to them and introduced itself.

The optimistic view of human reason and potential lay at the heart of Greek philosophy from the time of Plato and Aristotle, but its more modern manifestation can be seen in the period known as the Enlightenment (see Chapter 3). This eighteenth-century European philosophical movement, we recall, claimed that the power of human reason was sufficient to identify laws of science which would lead to human progress. It was argued that if oppression through organised and superstitious religion was curbed, largely through appropriate education, startling scientific, political and moral improvement would follow. And progress of a kind did seem to follow, thanks to the Industrial Revolution and the spread of science and technology in the Western world in the nineteenth and early twentieth centuries. This was the heroic age of the scientist: the objective, disinterested, white-coated seeker of truth before whom the laws of nature stood revealed. Small wonder that thinkers reacting for and against such changes looked for and claimed to find laws of progress in human society to match newly-discovered physical laws.

An influential 'science of society' was that of Karl Marx (see Chapter 4). We recall that Marx's explanation of change in history lies in the concept of 'class struggle'. Marx's friend and collaborator, Friedrich Engels, claimed that Marx's discovery of the law of development of human history was a scientific break-through comparable to Charles Darwin's theory of evolution.

The impact of Marx's thought is undeniable (see pages 80-81). But even those historians who reject Marxism and any form of model applied to the past should, in the view of postmodern theorists, be seen as modernist themselves. After all, they hold the view that intellectual study must be objective and concerned with 'reality'. The belief in disinterested scholarship and freedom of inquiry was and is part and parcel of Western liberal culture. And behind all this, of course, lay the modernist assumption that it was possible to identify reality and explain it to others.

Modernism is, of course, more than a set of intellectual attitudes. Religious ideals can be part of it. In fact, modernism is supposedly strong on codes of morality which are 'true' across time since they reflect 'eternal truths'. A feeling of optimism and even certainty about human progress can also be translated into an increased certainty about God's goodness, although one has to accept that there may well be a tension between faith, reason and science. Nevertheless, modernism in general is supposed to be characterised by the existence of optimism and a sense of certainty about what the human condition is and can be. It is possible for this to extend beyond the confines of the natural world into the world to come.

Examples of Modernism

The Age of Reason and the Enlightenment (see Chapter 3)
If we strip away the old superstitions like Catholicism and other types of organised religion, human reason can get to work to change the world. We can discover more and more about the way the world works and the way we as human beings work in it. Understanding the laws of human behaviour will lead to progress.

Marxism (see Chapter 4)
Human reason can identify the fundamental law which shapes our society. Society is shaped by technological change and the relationship between the different classes of people created by this change. The pattern we can identify throughout history is that of class struggle. We can predict future change because we have identified the law governing change.

Why, then, did some thinkers come to identify and so reject what they called modernism?

b) The Rejection of Modernism

i) The historical background

Our first theme should be a change in attitude towards our esteemed scientist. That technological advance - which owed so much to scientists - was not necessarily a good thing was starkly revealed by what machine guns could do to human bodies in the First World War. Some scientists were prepared to serve the cause of Nazism and even contribute towards providing the technology of genocide in the death camps. The atomic bomb attacks on Hiroshima and Nagasaki were all too obviously the products of scientific endeavour, and all too difficult to present as signs of optimism and progress. Neither was the evidence emanating from post-war Soviet Russia very comforting. That country had built up a massive technological and scientific establishment which had prostituted the ideals of scientific objectivity and had treated the environment and the living conditions of the people with scant regard. As historians of the 1960s turned their attention to the Western scientific establishments, it became clear that scientists, instead of being shut up in the laboratories in a suitably detached and objective manner, were anything but remote from the political, economic and social pressures surrounding the 'ordinary' citizen. Their science and even some of their 'results' and 'discoveries' were distorted by demands far different from those of truth. That historians should actually be looking at the issues of scientific objectivity is significant, and reflects a disenchantment with some of the seedier and more sinister aspects of capitalist Western culture: its racism and its readiness to impose itself on other cultures and countries through imperialism and colonialism. Many of those scholars important to postmodernist thought reacted strongly against the aggression of the Western powers, be it American involvement in Vietnam or French suppression and exploitation in her colony of Algeria. Of course, some people reacted against the capitalist West by following the thought of Marx. But there was plenty about the contemporary Communist States to object to as well. There was also the disillusionment following the failure of the May 1968 revolution in France where millions of workers had joined intellectuals and students in an attempt to overthrow de Gaulle's capitalist and imperialist Fifth Republic. The philosopher Roland Barthes commented on the failure of May 1968 in very significant terms:

> Make a revolution to destroy it, power will spring up again. And the reason why power is invincible is that the object in which it is carried for all human eternity is language: the language that we speak and write.[1]

Barthes' comments may seem unclear at this stage. Subsequent sections will help you get to grips with his reference to the importance of language and its relationship to power.

ii) Saussure, structuralism and language

A fundamental assumption of modernism was that language reflected our thought, which in turn reflected reality 'out there'. But the work of the Swiss linguist Ferdinand de Saussure (1857-1913) denied this. Language had a set of laws or structure, true enough (hence 'Structuralism'), but it operated by a system of signs which were not tied to an external reality. For example, take the English word 'sheep' and the French word 'mouton'. The word (or 'sign' in Saussure's terminology) 'sheep' conveys a particular meaning (Saussurean term, 'signifier') to the British: to the French, the word 'mouton', although clearly describing the same animal, has a subtly different meaning. This is because, in French, it means both the animal and the meat that comes from it. The British city dweller's view of sheep as attractive rural accessory would make no sense in French. So, meaning and words vary in an arbitrary way and reflect a different sense of reality. They cannot reflect a single, all-encompassing reality.

5 Poststructuralism

Poststructuralists accept with Structuralism the view that language did not reflect reality, but deny that there were any laws (even of the structuralist type) behind language. Yet, they argue, language is all we have to establish what we think is real. However, we must remember that we only think it is real: we have no way of accessing reality except through language, and language is incapable of doing it. This line of reasoning links conveniently with a dislike of the certainties of modernism and its assumptions that human reason can identify and therefore describe what is real, which, of course, the poststructuralists argued is impossible, given the limitations of language.

MODERNIST - We can identify and explain what is real.

POSTSTRUCTURALIST - We can do neither.

Poststructuralist historians therefore reject any theory of history which claims to identify or explain a law of development. In this way, poststructuralism is a variety of postmodernism. Both display what the French philosopher Lyotard called 'incredulity towards metanarratives'.[2] A metanarrative is not just a theory of historical change, but any type of framework which human reason imposes on the past (perhaps to explain or describe a development through time).

METANARRATIVE - The attempt to offer wide-ranging explanations by using reason, and expecting reason to be enough.

So, poststructuralism and postmodernism would object, not only to a typical Western liberal attempt to account for the rise and glory of parliament, but also to the Marxist law of history. As Robert Young puts it, 'poststructuralism challenges not just the politics and institutions of the right but also the politics and theoretical systems of the left'.[3]

What we now need to do is to look at some of the major intellectuals associated with poststructuralism to expand upon our understanding of the movement.

6 Jacques Derrida and Deconstruction

Deconstruction is a way of handling texts in which we do far more than try to understand what the author is saying. After all, Derrida (b.1930) argues that meaning itself is elusive. Language is full of signs which do not carry a single meaning: gaps, omissions, metaphors are just as important in establishing the various meanings there might be as the content is. The author is not in control of the language he uses because language does not operate on a series of rational rules. In fact, the author is absent from her or his text. There can be no one true reading of any text. You might think that this is an interesting way of looking at a poem or a novel, but Derrida argues that the technique applies to all texts. After all, it must do, since there is nothing outside the text. It is simply a false assertion of Western philosophy that there is a measurable, comprehensible reality against which texts can be judged. Texts are just based on other texts ('intertextuality'), and on nothing outside them.

What Derrida is doing is applying deconstruction to the standard texts of Western philosophy from Plato on down. In doing so, he claims to uncover not the workings of cool, calm reason and logic, but *rhetoric:* argument using the techniques of persuasion, like imagery and dominant metaphors, to convince the reader of a 'truth' which is not truth. Derrida also claims to identify within Western philosophical texts the unpleasant traits of ethnocentrism (seeing everything from the perspective of your culture, believing it to be superior to all others) and colonialism.

7 Michel Foucault and Power/Knowledge

Derrida has professed himself to be wary of history as a discipline and says little about it directly, although it was, in his view, subject to the same constraints of textuality as any other form of study. The French philosopher Foucault (1926-84) shared Derrida's poststructuralism, but wrote some works which are clearly historical in theme: *Madness and Civilisation* (1961); *The Birth of the Clinic: An Archaeology of Medical Perception* (1963); *Discipline and Punish* (1977); and the multi-volume *History of Sexuality* (from 1976).

Whilst Foucault accepted that language was not the communicator of reality, his main focus was how it communicated *power*. Power works through language by presenting a certain type of knowledge as if it were reality or truth. Let us take the way traditional historians claim that what makes sound historical writing is objectivity, allied to the calm application of reason and training in the historian's craft at university level. What is happening is that texts which do not match that particular model are attacked as unacceptable and the bearers of knowledge which is 'untrue'. So, upholding a particular system of knowledge is a tool for upholding power.

Foucault's *The Birth of the Clinic* is an attack on the standard assumptions made in the study of the history of medicine: namely, that modern medicine has triumphed over the alleged superstition and wild speculation of the irrational past. Modern medicine is, in this way, the heir to the objective, rational and progressive spirit of the Enlightenment. This rational system of knowledge (Foucault uses the word *epistime* for 'system of knowledge') is imposed by creating new categories of sickness, deviance or madness. Those who threaten to undermine the *epistime* are labelled as sick, deviant or mad and rendered powerless. What better method of tackling your opponents than having them seen as mad? But it is vital to understand that Foucault argues that power is not the product of government institutions, state control mechanisms or even individuals. It is spread throughout society, and has its home in language.

It should be clear from what has been said so far that it is typical of postmodernism/poststructuralism to see truth as relative - in other words, depending on different needs, different power relationships, different perspectives, rather than absolute, eternal, timeless. Many of Foucault's main concerns are summed up in the following passages:

> ... truth isn't outside power ... Each society has ... its régime of truth, its 'general politics' of truth: that is, the types of discourse which it accepts and makes function as true ... 'Truth' is linked ... with systems of power which produce and sustain it ...[4]

> I am well aware that I have never written anything but fictions.[5]

8 Hayden White

The American theorist and historiographer Hayden White has a perspective similar to that of Foucault. According to Georg Iggers, White argues that:

> an historical text is in essence nothing more than a literary text, a poetical creation as deeply involved in the imagination as the novel.[6]

White's book *Metahistory* (1973) offers an explanation of how he believes the historian puts a text together. His basic theory is that the content of the historian's work is as much invention as it is fact. White accepts that some of the raw material - the traces or original sources - may provide factual material, but such traces never provide a structure for these facts.

Only when the facts are given a structure by the historian do they make sense. So, there is a need for narrative - for story - to shape these traces and facts, and this is where the historian comes in. This shaping takes place firstly through the type of figurative language to be used (like irony, if the historian is disapproving). Then, he imposes on the traces of the past the type of argument which suits him (maybe Marxist style, for example). The argument is generally linked with what White calls 'emplotment' - the kind of story being told: romance, tragedy, comedy or satire. These four types of story are supposedly innate to the Western literary culture with which we are all familiar, and therefore help the story/history to make sense to the reader.

There seems to be a somewhat different emphasis here when one compares White to Derrida. To White, the author appears to be much more present in the text than in Derrida's deconstruction. Nevertheless, both clearly share the view that the past is not recoverable beyond the text, and that the text does not recover it anyway. There is no reality beyond the text to which one can appeal.

Summary Diagram
Postmodernist Ideas

Human reason cannot explain the past

Explanation can only take place through language. But our texts are full of gaps, symbols, metaphors and evasions of which even the writers are unaware.

The limits of human reason are shown by the behaviour of scientists. They should be disinterested seekers after the truth. In fact, they are the prisoners of their own language and political systems like the rest of us.

Most of the sources of history are texts. So, they are full of the same distortions. Historians cannot possibly uncover them all.

This is obvious from the way scientists have served Nazism and the atomic bomb programme.

Even if they could, their own texts would be distorted in exactly the same way.

So, the historian is really writing a form of fiction.

We can neither uncover nor explain what is absolutely and universally true. Truth is relative - relative to ourselves, to the various power-structures in our society. The 'truth' we uphold is the truth which best suits our needs.

9 A Critique of Postmodernism

It is quite straightforward to describe the main ideas of some of the major postmodernist thinkers, but evaluation is a different matter. The two-part central issue is: what impact does postmodernism have on the discipline called history, and is that impact to be welcomed?

a) History and Facts: E.H. Carr and G.R. Elton

There are a number of possible lines of attack on the postmodernist contention that the objective historian writing about the real past and doing so in a way which is 'truthful' is a modernist myth.

First, we need to look at the extent to which the writings of historians are based on 'facts' or 'events'. In fact, disagreement about this issue predates the contribution of postmodernism and forms a significant past of the so-called Carr-Elton debate. E.H. Carr's *What is History?* (first edition, 1961) took what at first sight seems like a near-postmodernist view of the relationship between history, the historian and the facts. Quite simply, Carr argued that written history is not governed and shaped by facts, but by the historian:

> It used to be said that facts speak for themselves. This is, of course, untrue. The facts speak only when the historian calls on them: it is he who decides to which facts to give the floor, and in what order or context.[7]

So, we must study the historian - his background, education, attitudes - before we can study what he had done to the facts. Carr expands upon this point by offering a definition of historical fact. When a fact from the past is included in an historical work, it is then subjected to the scrutiny of other historians. If it is widely accepted, then - and only then - does it become an historical fact. The point is that, as soon as the historian decides to pull it out from the mere facts of the past and converts it into an historical fact, it is inevitably part of an interpretation the historian imposes on the past. Carr put it this way:

> Its status as an historical fact will turn on a question of interpretation. This element of interpretation enters into every fact of history.[8]

The conservative historian G.R. Elton's response to this view in *The Practice of History* (1967) was simply to deny the interpretative element in historical facts. If, he said, an event can be known, then:

1   that is all that is required to make it a 'fact of history'. Interpretation, or general acceptance of a thesis, has nothing whatsoever to do with its independent existence. The point matters so much because Mr Carr, and others who like him think that history is what historians write, not

5   what happened, come dangerously close to suggesting either that it does not much matter what one says because (interpretation being

everything) there are always several reasonably convincing interpretations of any given set of events, or that history is altogether unknow-
able, being merely what happens to be said by a given historian at a
10 given moment.[9]

Elton was not simply saying that the historian's role is to collect and
present facts, although he does argue that there is a very large body of
what he calls 'agreed historical knowledge' on which the historian can
work. But in many cases, he said, the evidence itself is not clear-cut, or
there may be the need to select. Clearly the historian intervenes here,
but Elton denied that the historical facts are therefore so distorted
that one must accept Carr's view that studying the historian is a necessary preliminary to historical inquiry. Quite simply, Elton argued that
the 'cure' for the inevitable difficulties of the historian over the
partial nature of evidence and the allegation of subjectivity lies in the
'proper practice of scholarship and research.'
  So, Elton responded to the Carr challenge with two arguments:
1. That the methods of a trained, professional historian guard as
    effectively as possible against the distortions that some see as sepa-
    rating truth from history.
2. That the Carr approach denies the reality of historical knowl-
    edge, and is in this way a dangerous relativism. Relativism, we
    recall, is to deny that meaningful truth can be found, in that
    there are numbers of possible views, none of which can be proved
    to be the 'right' one.
I have spent some time over a debate which some would see as rather
out-of-date. But this is justified because Carr and Elton are sometimes
still presented as if they are the last word in the debate on the definition and meaning of history. More importantly, as we shall see, Elton's
argument based on the profession of history is often used to combat
the claims of the postmodernists themselves.
  One final point on Carr v. Elton. I suggested earlier that there were
clear similarities between Carr's standpoint and that of the postmodernists. However, there is one crucial difference. Despite what he had
to say about historical facts, Carr was not prepared to reject the possibility of the historian's objectivity. Instead, he came up with a very
curious argument. It seems that the objective historian is one who has
the right understanding of the pattern of development of history,
which includes an awareness of the likely shape of the future. Many
would agree with John Tosh that:

> Nothing is likely to be so subjective and value-laden as the projection of
> historical trends into the future, and Carr's attempt to do so with
> authority seems self-confident to the point of arrogance.[10]

Quite. But what I think is happening is not so much arrogance as a
rather desperate attempt to handle the danger of relativism. Carr did
not want to live with the full implications of his stance on the

unknowability of history through the inevitably subjective historian, since this would mean that many interpretations of history would have equal validity. Hence his curious, rather Marxist suggestion that the future can be predicted.

The link between a denial of the possibility of historical objectivity/accuracy and relativism is one we shall need to bear in mind. For the moment, I would like to pick up on Elton's argument about the way in which the professional skills and training of the historian offer a method of recovering something close to historical truth.

b) The Historian as Professional

In his Cook lectures of 1990 (published in 1991 as *Return to Essentials*), Elton used the model of the historian as professional-at-work against the postmodernists. He dismissed the postmodernist view of the essentially fictional nature of the historian's work by identifying the appropriate professional tools which the well-trained practitioner must use. Firstly, one must assume that the sources, traces, original documents, relics and so on do contain the truth: historians are bound by the authority of these sources. Secondly, one must approach the sources with a question in mind, but never seek a particular answer to it or distort the sources because historians have the advantage of hindsight (they know what happened next). In short, study the past on its own terms. Elton was not saying that, in an imperfect world, the historian can ever be completely objective. But he can guard himself against the dangers of reading into the past his own value-systems. Postmodernism, of course, argues that what the historian produces is inevitably present-minded (intentionally or not). Elton responded:

> For the historian is in the first place concerned with the people of the past - with their experiences, thoughts and actions - and not with the people of the present, least of all with himself.[11]

What emerges from the historian's efforts will not be the whole truth, but it will have the strong flavour of it.

The stance of Arthur Marwick is very similar. In his introductory textbook *The Nature of History* (third edition, 1989), he provides a numbered list of questions the professional historian asks (instinctively or otherwise) of the primary sources, ranging from the probing of authenticity, provenance (where the source comes from), type of source, the position of the author and so on. His rather bad-tempered contribution to Kozicki's *Developments of Modern Historiography* (1993) includes a similar focus on the historian's technique. Marwick attacks the postmodernist stance of Anthony Easthope, who argues that no-one can claim a knowledge of reality since that reality - and their own responses to it - are the creation of discourse (the language of the text). Marwick responds by asserting that reality does exist in the primary sources, and draws a significant distinction between primary and secondary sources:

> History's critics need to appreciate that there is a crucial distinction between *primary* sources ... and *secondary* sources, the history which historians produce through the systematic, disciplined, study of the primary sources.[12]

But have Marwick and Elton succeeded in convincing us that they are right to reject postmodernist approaches to facts, sources and the partly-recapturable reality of history? Frankly, not really. The main problem is that, when you compare the pair to, say, Foucault or White, they seem to be talking about different things. Essentially, the Marwick/Elton approach is technical, profession-based: their frequent complaint is that their opponents do not know what they are talking about because they are not true, practising historians. But White and company are talking about history not as a craft or set of specific techniques, but in terms of epistemology: in other words, looking at history as a theory of knowledge and analysing its claims to provide true knowledge about the past. The Marwick/Elton critique simply whizzes over the heads of its target, because it never really gets to grips with the main points of the postmodernist arguments. This is very clear when we look at Hayden White's response to Marwick's article.[13]

White points out that he is perfectly happy to accept that events have a reality. What he is disputing is that 'facts' (which he clearly separates from 'events') are anything other than a fundamentally fictional construction - either in the documents or in historians' texts. They are, in fact, 'linguistic entities' which are inevitably subject to change as our attitudes to what are facts change. So, he is presumably denying that anything mentioned by an historian beyond the straight-forward event and its date can be seen as 'true'. And some of those influenced by postmodernism seem unwilling to allow the possibility of knowing any past reality whatsoever.

c) Other Objections to Postmodernist Approaches

So - is it possible to respond to postmodernist claims without resorting to a list of the historian's techniques? I believe that it is, and on a number of levels. First of all, we need to look at the issue of the relationship between text and reality. In postmodernist terms, language creates reality: there is no distinction between historical writing and fiction. Perhaps so: but the argument depends upon the acceptance of a linguistic theory (initially, that of Saussure) which is not necessarily true and which is by no means universally accepted as such by linguists themselves. Secondly, there is a logical problem - a contradiction - in Derridean deconstruction. Remember that Derrida proclaims the undiscoverability of a single, 'true' meaning in text and denies the author's control over it. Derrida, we recall, accompanies deconstruction with an attack on the use of reason in Western philosophy. Yet, he uses reason and logic to denounce reason and logic. This hardly seems reasonable, logical or fair. Also, deconstruction rejects the standard historical technique of contextualising a source: in other words, Derrida denies that there is any point in looking at the social, economic, political, ideological and personal background in order to understand the author's meaning. But is this really acceptable? Suppose one were studying one of the notorious anti-Semitic passages from Hitler's *Mein Kampf.* Deconstruction would have us locate the gaps, silences, metaphors and secrets within the text, but would deny that it reflects the author's meaning. It would deny us the opportunity to help explain the text by reference to widespread anti-semitic ideas, Hitler's experiences in Vienna and so on. The meaning of words cannot be divorced from the environment in which they are used. Just because one can detect within a text the silences, gaps and so on it does not mean that there is nothing else there. To say that some of an historian's work has a fictional element to it is not to deny that reasoned explanation is also there. To do so would be throwing out the baby with the bath-water.

One scholar who has gained much from postmodernism is Edward Said, but he is now keen to stress that postmodern theorists have been too squeamish about relating their findings to the world outside the text. In *The World, the Text and the Critic,* Said comments:

1   My position is that texts are worldly, to some degree they are events,
    and, even when they appear to deny it, they are nevertheless a part of
    the social world, human life ... The realities of power and authority - as
    well as the resistances offered [to them] ... are the realities that make
5   texts possible ...[14]

Perhaps the most serious objection to postmodernism concerns its relativism. The denial that the writing of historians contains an objective reality - or that there is an objective reality one can communicate through language and which can be used to assess the quality of an historian's work - means that there is no way of judging such work as 'true' or 'untrue'. Some enthusiasts see this as a positive good. Keith Jenkins feels that those who complain about the absence of criteria of judgement are afraid of losing their élitist positions as arbiters of what 'correct' history is. According to him, the collapse of the old meta-narratives and modernist certainties is liberating. Postmodernism will encourage the spread of many-voiced history, as people of all types write local, national, regional histories - whatever, in fact, meets their needs. If it does meet their needs, all well and good. The only thing they cannot do is to claim it as 'true'.

I find this approach deeply worrying. First of all, it seems to me to be as much a reflection of free-market Western capitalism - go out and buy yourself a history - as it is a reflection of a theory of epistemology.

Secondly, denial of a 'true' history plays into the hands of those who have a vested interest in a denial of their own - namely, that the Holocaust actually happened. What postmodernism does is to accept the right of neo-Nazis and others to claim that the genocide of six million Jews never took place, and at the same time sabotages the right of those who oppose them to appeal to the 'truth'. Postmodernism would have us believe that countless eyewitness reports, the sufferings of survivors, the testimonies of death camp guards and commandants, the evidence from film and the writings of historians which make use of them all are not enough to constitute the truth. This is not a train I personally care to ride, and I can only advise those who have enjoyed the postmodernist trip so far to get off now. As Richard Evans says, Auschwitz was not a discourse; nor were gas chambers a piece of rhetoric. In short, 'it trivialises mass murder to see it as a text.'[15] Indeed.

The postmodernist theoreticians do not, in my view, rise to that challenge posed by the Holocaust. The moral dangers of White's relativism and the issue of Nazism are barely touched on in Jenkins. In a footnote, he comments that:

> It seems to me that whether we like it or not the kind of relativism which White articulates is a fact of life.[16]

Well, I do not like it, and it does not seem to me to be a fact of life (whatever that means). Jenkins' curious certainties about uncertainty are hardly a substitute for argument, although they are very much part of his rhetoric. He tells us that we live in a postmodern world, that we have no widely-held systems of belief or 'centres' anymore - really? Is this actually the case, or are we simply being invited to visit the planet Jenkins, and feel at home?

We should conclude our critique by summarising the impact postmodernist approaches have on the writing of history. Whatever our stance on postmodernism, it has to be said that there has been very little by way of postmodernist works of history (as opposed to theory) on which to base comments. Foucault's works are perhaps the closest we get. But on what grounds does one evaluate them? In terms of traditional history, with its demands for proof, analysis of cause and effect, Foucault's work is a non-starter. Nor does he trouble to make his meaning clear: a not-uncommon postmodernist failing. A more recent example would be Simon Schama's *Dead Certainties* (1991), which, set in eighteenth and nineteenth-century North America, is more imaginative reconstruction using the techniques of the novelist than a recognisable work of history.

The issue of postmodernist works of history is tackled by Jenkins, in a chapter entitled 'Doing history in the post-modern world'. Sadly, he devotes very little space to the actual form it might take, but comes up with the following:

1 If the present can best be understood as post-modern ... then this
   suggests to me that the content of a preferred history should be studies
   of this phenomenon ... In the post-modern world, then, arguably the
   content and context of history should be a generous series of method-
5 ologically reflexive studies of the makings of the histories of post-
   modernity itself.[17]

This means (I think) that we have before us the prospect of writing
postmodern histories about postmodern histories. Not unduly
enticing, perhaps. Unbelievably limiting, most certainly. The main
problem with this is that it ignores completely what may well be the
basic human need for historical explanation. It is an old argument
(but a good one) to claim that history - particularly historical narrative - offers us the chance to locate ourselves through a sense of
shared local and national identity. Historical narrative offers us a
necessary help with understanding our political, economic, cultural
and social present which 'methodologically reflexive studies of the
makings of the histories of post-modernity itself' may not do so well
(if at all). I very much like Appleby's conclusion on this point:

1 The move toward the most radically sceptical and relativist postmodern
   position inevitably leads us into a cul-de-sac. Dismissals of history, politics, and narrative as hopelessly modern ideas, now outmoded in the
   postmodern world, might seem up-to-date, but history, politics, and
5 narrative are still the best tools available for dealing with the world and
   preparing for the future.[18]

d) Politics and Postmodernism

One charge against postmodernism is that it discourages political
involvement and action. After all, it rejects political theories like
Marxism as hopelessly modernist. And it cultivates a liberal, rather
ironic and perhaps mocking stance which is good at deconstruction
but no help in construction. Foucault's view of power as all-pervasive
in effect makes political action difficult to engage in because there is
no obvious target for it. If power were simply embodied in the state, or
in one class, then one would have something tangible to fight against.

Summary
Arguments Against Postmodernist History

Postmodernists attack the assumption of Western philosophy that
human reason and logic can be used to uncover truth. But their
attack makes use of the very reason and logic they wish to deny.

A typical postmodernist position seems to be that 'It is true to say that there is no truth'. A paradox, perhaps?

The attack on language as a way of communicating reality is based upon a theory in linguistics which is very much open to challenge. In any case, to claim it as universally valid is just to set up the kind of all-embracing theory that postmodernists denounce.

Postmodernist relativism is a useful weapon for those who deny the truth of the Holocaust. To deny the reality of Auschwitz is to fly in the face of acceptable morality and common sense. I can appreciate that common sense is an awkward concept for the historian to use, since what is common sense to one age is not necessarily common sense to another. But I think that any age confronted by the wealth of evidence that Auschwitz was a death camp would accept it as true. Explanations of why it was a death camp might differ, of course.

Postmodernism offers no explanation for change in history, and would discourage anyone believing in the need for change from trying to achieve it.

Postmodernism would deny that any one explanation of causes is better than any other, because there is no universally valid criteria by which to judge. This is unfortunate. There is surely a need for explanation of causes which would do more than satisfy the prejudices of a particular interest group. The Holocaust is again the obvious example here. The belief that genocide is fundamentally wrong is spread across national and cultural boundaries, and therefore an explanation of how it could occur can and should make sense across the same boundaries. That explanation must be meaningful to Germans, the British, the French, North Americans and to the world at large. I am not saying that simplistic lessons can be learned (see my concluding chapter) but that historians cannot abandon a very real obligation to explain causes in as objective a way as possible. If they do not, then others will offer explanations that could be profoundly dangerous.

10 Positive Postmodernism

So far, I have described the main ideas of the postmodernism and postmodernists. I then pointed out what seemed to me to be the defects in postmodernist approaches to history. But I want to emphasise that, if we avoid some of the more extreme and relativistic stances, postmodernism is a healthy blast of air in the dustier corridors of historiography. In this section, I shall concentrate on some of the more useful aspects.

i) Texts and postmodernism

Although I did not accept the full rigours of the postmodernist position on textuality, this is not to dismiss the value of its insights. If we interrogate a text in a Derridean manner, then our understanding of it is significantly increased. The images chosen, the evasions dictated by social taboos, the unwitting as well as the intentional content: all these provide the historian (particularly the cultural historian, perhaps) with useful insights. If we stop short of denying that the author and reader have any control over meaning, then there is much here to be gained. Saying that, of course, is one thing: what we need are examples. I have chosen two very different works to illustrate the positive appeal of postmodernist strategies.

Firstly, I am going to look at a work edited by Averil Cameron which deals with the value of postmodernist strategies in ancient history: *History as Text: The Writing of Ancient History.* Significantly, Cameron comments that, generally, ancient historians have operated on the lines of Elton in fighting shy of postmodernism. Nevertheless, there are, it appears, things to be learned from a postmodernist approach to textuality. In her chapter 'Virginity as Metaphor: women and the rhetoric of early Christianity', Cameron explains the difficulty of trying to recapture women's experience from the early Christian texts. Close analysis of the texts shows that what we see is not only a male rhetoric presenting women as dangerous through their sexuality: we also see that the male writer's language is aimed at exerting power and control. The male-dominated Church needed discipline, authority and social respectability to survive, and so its rhetoric attacked what it saw as those who were potentially dangerous: and that included women. Cameron, in analysing the literary/rhetorical devices of the texts, is going beyond both the mechanical extracting of information from the source and also the standard method of putting it into the context of contemporary theological ideas. Her method is clearly fruitful. She is able to identify the rhetoric within a well-known text on the early woman Saint Perpetua which turns her into an 'honorary man … while at the same time continuing to observe the boundaries placed on female behaviour by men'.[19] Historians treating the apparently simple and straightforward account of Perpetua's martyrdom as essentially factual (and approving of women) are therefore in danger, not only of being misled, but also of missing the way in which the text imposes power and control.

Cameron is not accepting the full weight of Derridean deconstruction here. In her Postlude, she is clearly concerned that history must not be seen only as a mode of rhetoric - a fictional text. There are, she argues, tried and tested methods of checking the truth of historical narratives, and that truth is not the 'truth' as presented in a novel. In any case, Cameron's work includes the kind of contextualising that postmodernists would dismiss.

ii) Edward Said and 'Orientalism'

My second example is from the work of Edward Said. Said's *Orientalism,* as suggested earlier, owes much to Foucault's power/knowledge concept. Said is looking at the links between Western theories of imperialism and the way imperialism operated in practice. The West has claimed to know what the true Orient is (and what the true Oriental is like), but this 'knowledge' simply meets the needs of power and control: it justifies colonialism. The Western imperialist claims to know the Oriental better than he knows himself, and can see in him an irrationality, a childishness, an untrustworthiness which needs to be channelled (in his own interest, of course) by the rational, adult, trustworthy Westerner. Said opens his book with a discussion of a speech made by the former British Prime Minister A.J. Balfour to the House of Commons in 1910. Balfour is replying to a complaint from an MP about the British government's involvement in Egypt and about his tone of superiority in talking about the Orient in general:

1   I take up no attitude of superiority. But I ask [anyone] … who has even the most superficial knowledge of history, if they will look in the face the facts with which a British statesman has to deal when he is put in a position of supremacy over great races like the inhabitants of Egypt and
5   countries in the East. We know the civilisation of Egypt better than we know the civilisation of any other country. We know it further back; we know it more intimately; we know more about it … Western nations as soon as they emerge into history show the beginnings of those capacities for self-government … You may look through the whole history of
10   the Orientals … and you will never find traces of self-government … Is it a good thing for these great nations - I admit their greatness - that this absolute government should be exercised by us? I think it is a good thing. I think that experience shows that they have got under it far better government than in the whole history of the world they ever had
15   before …'[20]

Said points to the obvious link being made by Balfour between knowledge of the Orient and power over it. Said is not saying anything as simplistic as 'Politicians came up with Orientalism in order to justify their colonialism', because Orientalism - the belief in the 'otherness' of the Orient - predated colonial and imperial expansion. In any case, as with Foucault, he is arguing that the power relationship is imbedded in language itself, and language is not the prisoner of statesmen.

It is at this point, however, that we hit a problem. Said has to admit that all knowledge, including his own academic knowledge, is distorted by this power-relationship between the West and the Orient.

As we saw earlier, this, in theory, makes it difficult to use the full weight of Foucault's ideas in any attempt to create political change. In short, how can his texts, which are bound to reflect the power relationships in his own society, somehow step outside those power relationships to subvert them? As Robert Young points out,[21] Said tries to fight against Orientalism by appealing to what he calls the 'human spirit'. And what is this spirit? It turns out to be little more than the best elements of the very Western culture which contains and transmits Orientalism - writers like Thomas Hardy or James Joyce - who supposedly possess the ability to resist power and oppression. In arguing in this way, Said has to reject Foucault's dismissal of the importance of the effect of individuals on history.

All criticisms taken into account, *Orientialism* is a superb book: lucid, wide-ranging, immensely thought-provoking. Its use of postmodernist approaches to textuality and power/knowledge reveals the dominant colonial discourse in operation. It also exposes some of the weaknesses in postmodernism, including the failure to take account of individual impact on history and an absence of any method of encouraging change in existing power-relationships.

11 Postmodernism and the Historian's Objectivity

As we approach the end of the Chapter, I want to look at a question which is often raised in discussions on the nature of history: how far can historians be objective? Seeking answers to this question will also provide a useful reminder of many postmodernist arguments.

In postmodernist terms, the notion of the objective historian is a) a joke and b) just the product of a modernist way of thinking. Objectivity is impossible for a number of reasons. Firstly, it presupposes that the truth about the past is recoverable. The postmodernist response is that it is not, since we are all prisoners of the fluidity of language, and we have no way of recapturing the past other than through language. Meaning is not fixed: neither we nor the authors of the texts we study are able to control meaning. Secondly, objectivity is a modernist claim which might have suited the old certainties of Western liberalism and Marxism, but is now totally outmoded (and exposed as such) in our postmodern era. Thirdly, those who claim objectivity also often claim to be letting the past speak for itself. This is rubbish. History is never neutral - it is always for someone.

Against this, we recall, Elton and Marwick set out the specific professional skills of the historian, which, in their view, effectively sift the truth and guard against his inevitable prejudices and biases. I use the word 'inevitable' advisedly, because not even Elton would argue that the historian can exclude himself totally from the sources and his work on them. However, this involvement is not dominance: '... it does not mean ... that he cannot escape from his prejudices and preconceptions'.[22]

Now, I had cause to criticise both Elton and Marwick for failing to answer the philosophical arguments of the postmodernists. I then suggested that there were serious objections to postmodernist assumptions about the unknowability of the past and the lack of meaning in language. But I also suggested that historians had much to gain from postmodern insights and techniques on textuality so long as historians did not accept that the author is absent. Postmodernism, in fact, helps us to identify in a sophisticated way the rhetoric in all texts, including our own. We must be prepared to accept - much more than Elton would - that the historian employs many of the devices of fiction, and be aware of it. We must be prepared to accept - much more than Elton would - that our language is often dominated by power, and that the way we discuss things may well reflect the dominant discourse and the particular type of knowledge that is accepted as 'true'.

Of course, one might argue that this is all very well for assessing the writing of historians - the secondary sources. But a good historian is going to work with - perhaps base his work on - the primary evidence (or traces), and so all the dire warnings about textuality do not apply. But this argument (resting as it does on a Marwick-style separation of primary and secondary sources) seems quite wrong. After all, texts of all types are distorted in just the same way as the historian's own writing. However, we should be aware that historians, however traditional and dismissive of postmodernism, frequently treat their sources in a way which is similar to deconstruction. Very often, the value of a source rests in the unwitting testimony: the value-systems, the assumptions about social class or family life, that the author of the source never bothers articulating because they are taken for granted. Historians are used to looking for this kind of thing, and I can see no reason to argue that their efforts are going to be sabotaged by the original text or their own biases, as long as they are aware of them.

Looking back over the last two paragraphs, I notice the number of times I used the word 'aware'. This, perhaps, is the key to the question of objectivity. After all, objectivity is less a personal quality or attribute than an awareness of the difficulties of being objective. If one takes those difficulties into account, then something at least approaching objectivity becomes possible. So, the historian needs to be aware of the following:

i) The text the historian writes will be subject to his own evasions, biases, silences, relationships to power and the type of knowledge legitimised by authority. His rhetoric may distort his text. It may, for example, portray a fake objectivity by resolutely refusing to use the word 'I'.

ii) The primary sources will be subject to some or all of the same distortions.

iii) The past may be recreated only in the mind of the historian, but its shape cannot and should not be the product of that mind. The historian, in short, can recognise when he is shaping it for his own purposes - largely because the traces of the past genuinely reflect its reality and its 'otherness'. Accept this, and one can guard against the distorting of the past.

iv) The historian must approach the past with questions, but also be aware of the danger of dictating the answers the past gives. Against this, it is sometimes argued that the sources are mute, and what they appear to articulate is only what the historian wants them to say. This is a superficially attractive argument, but one which misinterprets the process of source evaluation. This process is best seen as a dialogue, where the historian approaches the source with his question (which is probably part of an hypothesis). That hypothesis is measured against the evidence provided by the sources (their reply) and tentatively confirmed, modified or rejected in the light of that answer: and so the process continues. I like E.P. Thompson's discussion of this approach, which rests on what he calls 'historical logic':

> By 'historical logic' I mean a logical method of enquiry appropriate to historical materials, designed as far as possible to test hypotheses as to structure, causation, etc., and to eliminate self-confirming procedures ('instances', 'illustrations'). The disciplined historical discourse of the proof consists in a dialogue between concept and evidence, a dialogue conducted by successive hypotheses, on the one hand, and empirical research on the other. The interrogator is historical logic ... the respondent is the evidence, with its determinate properties.[23]

Thompson's last sentence is particularly important: note his point that the evidence, in the end, determines the outcome of the dialogue.

v) One should remember that total impartiality is as unlikely as the recovery of the total truth about the past.

vi) When the cry for objectivity is yoked to a demand that the 'sources be left to speak for themselves', it may simply reflect a conservative ideological position and therefore a fear of change. This is because it may in turn reflect a denial that the present can ever use the past to help solve its own problems, on the grounds that each age is unique and should simply be allowed to speak (see Chapter 3, pages 58-59)

vii) Objectivity is not a plant one can cultivate alone. It is encouraged by the community of scholars, where research is the subject of careful scrutiny.

viii) Be aware, not only of the dangers of overstating the possibilities of objectivity, but also the dangers of denying it completely. The effect of dismissing objectivity as hopelessly old-fashioned and modernist is to put a foot on the slippery slope of relativism.

Since awareness is all, I should make it clear that I am aware that my comments on the possibility of achieving something meaningful (if imperfect) in terms of objectivity have ended up being similar to those of Elton and Marwick (and the left-wing historian Thompson). The difference is that I claim to have at least considered the epistemological attack of postmodernism in a more meaningful way than Elton and Marwick, and also to have recognised its real merits. And I do not think I lost my temper in their manner. The late Sir Geoffrey Elton was inimitable in this, as in many other ways. He says:

> ... we [meaning 'real' historians] are fighting for the lives of innocent young people beset by devilish tempters [the postmodernists] who claim to offer higher forms of thought and deeper truths and insights - the intellectual equivalent of crack, in fact.[24]

If nothing else, Elton's words certainly justify that image of battle with which I started the chapter.

12 Conclusion

In his book *Re-thinking History*, Keith Jenkins bravely offers a brief definition of history at the end of his chapter 'What history is'. This is an excellent idea, and I make no excuse for doing exactly the same thing. After I have offered my definition, you may care to read what Jenkins has to say from his enthusiastically postmodern perspective. This is my definition:

1 History does not exist in the present: it cannot be recreated for us to observe or experience. It exists largely through the writings of historians, who inevitably distort it to a greater or lesser degree. The distortion takes place for some or all of the following reasons:-

5   i) The traces from the past are never complete.

      ii) The historian is likely to be influenced by his academic training, the prevailing systems of power and authority in his society, his political and religious beliefs, social class and the pressures to publish work as a criteria for success.

10   iii) All texts, including those used by the historian and those produced by the historian, contain a range of complexities stemming from the nature of language. These will include elements which are rhetorical/fictional, deliberate or unintentional omissions, unwitting testimony.

15   Nevertheless, the competent historian who is aware of these distortions can offer an account based on the traces and historians' interpretations to satisfy the very real need of his society for an explanation of the past which is grounded in reality, even if it cannot claim to communicate the absolute truth.

And here is Jenkins' version:

1 History is a shifting, problematic discourse, ostensibly about an aspect of the world, the past, that is produced by a group of present-minded workers (overwhelmingly in our culture salaried historians) who go

about their work in mutually recognisable ways that are ... method-
5 ologically, ideologically and practically positioned and whose products,
once in circulation, are subject to a series of uses and abuses that are
logically infinite but which in actuality generally correspond to a range
of power bases that exist at any given moment and which structure and
distribute the meanings of histories along a dominant-marginal spec-
trum.[25]

I hope you will have noted the similarities and differences in the two
versions - if you have not, it will be worthwhile re-reading the definitions in order to do so. The war over the definition of history will most
definitely rumble on, thank goodness. It is a healthy sign when those
involved in studying history are obliged to think about the nature of
their own discipline, even if it is a pity that entrenched positions are
sometimes defended with bile. If I may use the military metaphor for
one last time, I would like to claim that I have raised my head above
the parapet sufficiently to appreciate the good points in the various
strategies. But I do not claim to be an entirely neutral observer. Who
would want to be stuck in no-man's land?

References

1 R. Barthes in S. Sontag (ed.), *A Barthes Reader* (Cape, 1982), p.459.
2 J-F. Lyotard, *The Postmodern Condition* (Manchester University Press, 1984), p.xxiv.
3 R. Young, *White Mythologies. Writing History and the West* (Routledge, 1990), pp.1-2.
4 M. Foucault, *Power/Knowledge. Selected Interviews and Other Writings, 1972-1977* (Harvester, 1980), pp.131-3.
5 M. Foucault, quoted in L. Hunt (ed.), *The New Cultural History* (University of California Press, 1989), p.8.
6 Georg G. Iggers, in H. Kozicki (ed.), *Developments in Modern Historiography* (Macmillan, 1993), p.3.
7 E.H. Carr, *What is History?* (Penguin, second edition, 1987), p.11.
8 Ibid., pp.12-13.
9 G.R. Elton, *The Practice of History* (Fontana, 1969), p.76.
10 J. Tosh, *The Pursuit of History* (Longman, second edition, 1984), p.148.
11 G.R. Elton, *Return to Essentials* (Cambridge University Press, 1991), p.43.
12 Marwick, in Kozicki, *Developments*, p.136.
13 Hayden White, 'Response to Arthur Marwick', ibid., pp.233-46.
14 E.W. Said, *The World, the Text and the Critic* (Vintage, 1983), pp.4-5.
15 Evans, *In Defence of History*, (Granta, 1997), p.124.
16 K. Jenkins, *On 'What is History?'* (Routledge, 1995), p.192.
17 K. Jenkins, *Re-thinking History* (Routledge, 1991) p.70.
18 J. Appleby, L. Hunt, M. Jacob, *Telling the Truth about History* (Norton, 1995), p.236.
19 A. Cameron (ed.), *History as Text. The Writing of Ancient History* (Duckworth, 1989), p.194.

20 E. Said, *Orientalism* (Penguin, 1995), pp.32-3.
21 R. Young, *White Mythologies: Writing History and the West* (Routledge, 1990). See pp.132-4.
22 Elton, *Return to Essentials*, p.43.
23 E.P. Thompson, *The Poverty of Theory and Other Essays* (Merlin, 1978), p.39.
24 Elton, *Return to Essentials*, p.41.
25 Jenkins, *Re-thinking History*, p.26.

Making notes on 'Defining History'

This chapter, we recall, does not seek to provide students with the basic material for the standard questions in A level-type examinations. Instead, it is here to encourage inquisitive students to consider issues which complement that material. Detailed notes are therefore not needed. I suggest that those who want to give that added dimension to essays make use of the summary diagrams on page 120 and pages 127-128 and the section below.

Answering essay questions on 'Defining History'

It is likely that the ideas discussed in this chapter will be used to supplement what you have to say in essays on the value of history (see the concluding chapter) or in essays on historiographical issues such as 'letting the past speak' (Chapter 3). However, for those who wish to be sure that they have fully mastered this difficult material, I would advise attempting the following question:

'Postmodernism applied to the study and writing of history is a dangerous drug; and, like a dangerous drug, it must be avoided at all costs.' To what extent do you agree with this view?

As you know, it always vital to identify the key words in a question and, where necessary, to offer a definition of them in the introductory paragraph of your essay. This should - if you do it carefully - suggest to the examiner that you have read the question properly and are going to address it directly. The obvious word requiring such a definition in this question is 'postmodernism'. But you must relate it to its effect on history, rather than launch into an explanation which is largely descriptive. So, you might like to consider the effect of postmodernism on the traditional discipline of history. Listed below you will find four of the standard assumptions made by most historians. Try to explain the postmodern perspective on each of them.

1. Historians collect evidence from the past. They assume that this evidence contains truth, which can be extracted by the usual techniques of source evaluation.
2. Historians claim to be able to explain the past rationally without distorting it to suit their own needs.

3. Historians assume that there are wrong interpretations of the past, as well as those which are closest to the truth.
4. Historians claim to write fact rather then fiction.

If you have been able to offer the postmodernist perspective on each of these, you should have recognised that your argument is beginning to take shape. It is certainly true that postmodernism will undermine all of these cherished assumptions, and that the statement in the question appears to be one which you could support. But can you support it fully? These kinds of question always demand a for/against or 'on the one hand'/ 'on the other hand' approach. Can you not make use of the Positive Postmodernism paragraphs to avoid rejecting postmodernism altogether?

Source-based questions on 'Defining History'

Read the extract from Keith Jenkins on pages 134-135 and answer the following questions.
a) What does Jenkins mean when he speaks of history being a 'shifting, problematic discourse'? (5 marks)
b) Discuss, with examples chosen from previous chapters, Jenkins' view that historians are inevitably 'ideologically positioned'. (10 marks)
c) Write a detailed critique of Jenkins' arguments on the nature of history. (10 marks)

In answering question b), I suggest you consider in particular those historians who are often praised for their scholarly approach and objectivity. Bede and Ranke would seem to be good candidates. You will need to discuss the extent to which Bede's work is distorted by his 'evangelical purpose' and how Ranke's position may be seen to reflect his conservative political stance and Lutheran beliefs. But remember also that the assessment of Ranke was by no means dismissive of his objectivity. A key section to make use of in your answer is section 11. I would strongly advise you to draw up a plan for this question, using the 'on the one hand'/ 'on the other hand' format.

6 Conclusion: Types of Explanation and the Value of History

Those who expect conclusions to be mere summaries of arguments already presented are going to be disappointed by this one. But then, a decent conclusion should, perhaps, encourage readers to think about those arguments from new perspectives and in a broader context. And so, we are going to pick up and expand upon two themes which have been woven into the previous chapters. Firstly, we will examine the different types of explanation offered by historians, using the familiar and helpful distinction between narrative and analytical history. Secondly, we are going to tackle the issue of the purpose and value of history. Some historians, we recall, were keen explicitly to identify a purpose in writing history - to teach moral and political lessons. Whether it can do so is an issue worthy of discussion. But it would be quite wrong to limit ourselves to historiography. Should we not also consider the value of history to those who do not read the works of historians?

1 Types of Explanation in History: Defining Narrative and Analytical History

I   Miss Wedgwood has been working for many years on her most ambi-
    tious work, the tremendous story of the Great Rebellion which cost
    King Charles I his life and turned England into a republic. The King's Peace
    is the first act of this great historic drama … It tells the story of the
5   four eventful years which immediately preceded the Civil War … her
    intention is not so much to analyse the causes of the Civil War as to
    understand how the men and women of that time thought and felt, and
    why, in their own estimation, they acted as they did.[1]

Veronica Wedgwood wrote narrative history, and many of its most typical characteristics are ably outlined in the above blurb from the 1974 edition of *The King's Peace*. Narrative history focuses on political events, and generally seeks to explain how events came about by concentrating on the actions of individuals - typically, the motives of the élites in whose hands political, social and economic power was concentrated. In short, its analysis of causation would be limited. The assumption that events were shaped largely by the decisions of individuals generally leads to the down-playing of impersonal and longer-term causes such as changes in power-relationships or in the economic structures of society. Political and diplomatic history lends itself to narrative, but it is hard to see how story-type narration can cope with an in-depth analysis of the causes of a major transformation in society (like the Industrial Revolution) or the issues reflecting the expanded scope of twentieth-century historical writing, such as the history of silence, of death, or the history of mentalities.

Analytical history, however, tackles problems rather than story. Its explanation relies less on human agency (the actions of individuals) than it does on a detailed discussion of the fundamental structures of society - its institutions, economic foundations and modes of thought.

2 Applying the Definitions of Narrative and Analytical History

The aim is now to apply the model of the distinction between narrative and analytical history to the historians studied in previous chapters. Narrative history concentrating on the impact of individuals was a marked characteristic of much of the work of the classical and Renaissance historians. Herodotus spoke of the accomplishing of astonishing deeds and gave some shape to his work by emphasising the way in which chains of loyalty and revenge themselves shaped events. As befitted a military commander, Thucydides was fascinated by the psychology of war. Roman historians used rhetoric as a vital tool in outlining noble deeds to be emulated and evil deeds to be shunned. Polybius, however, appears to have offered a more analytical approach. He stressed the importance of the Roman 'mixed' constitution, whose system of checks and balances allowed it, for a time, to escape the pattern of growth and decay which Polybius claimed to have identified in history. In practice, this focus on structures was compromised. When discussing wars, Polybius tended to ignore the longer-term causes in favour of rather superficial references to the anger of a people, or the confidence bred of success. He was unable to relate the personal to the structural, as he lacked a feel for the to-and-fro of political life in Rome: the analysis of the structure of the constitution was not complemented by an effective discussion of its relationship to actual political behaviour.

Medieval Christian historians did not find a cyclical pattern of growth and decay at all to their taste. Their vision of history was essentially linear: from the creation to Christ, and from Christ to His anticipated Second Coming. Explanation was, in the case of Bede, harnessed to the need to evangelise the pagan and to feed the faith of the converted. God intervened directly in the affairs of the world to reward the faithful and to punish His enemies. Later medieval historians did not need to counter the long-vanished threat of paganism within their own lands, but their superficial narratives continue to root descriptions of causes of major and minor events in terms of reward for faith and good deeds and punishment for sin.

The Renaissance historians were generally able to translate their devotion to the classical historians into narratives with a fundamentally Christian moral framework. The exception, we recall, was Machiavelli. Not for him was the story-style history with suitably Christian moral examples. His explanations were profoundly secular, and based upon an analysis of the structure of the Roman constitution. In his *Discourses on Livy*, he argued, like Polybius, that civic leaders should use religion as a military and political tool to inspire confidence in battle and to prevent selfish and anti-social behaviour. Machiavelli was not recommending the use of religion because it was true. He even reversed the standard Christian assumption that peace was a good in itself by praising class conflict as a mechanism for maintaining political stability, commenting that good laws derived from disturbances between nobles and plebeians that 'many people thoughtlessly condemn'.

Machiavelli, then, was writing history that was essentially secular, analytical and unrepresentative of his time. However, he did share with his contemporaries the assumption that human nature did not change as society changed through time. This was also a characteristic of most of the *philosophes*, whose historical writing converted these assumptions into optimistic generalisations about the human spirit and, in effect, into laws of human behaviour. A right understanding of these laws - unobscured by religious dogma - would lead to progress for humanity. *Philosophes* writing history were able to move beyond the standard Renaissance obsession with political and military history and moral example into analyses of manners, laws, constitutions and customs. However, it would be unwise to proffer Gibbon as an example of the typical Enlightenment historian. His great work, *History of the Decline and Fall of the Roman Empire*, is not a fundamentally analytical work focused on causation: it is largely a narrative in which Gibbon invited the reader to enter into a dialogue - mind to mind - in an exploration of the events and personalities of the past: but it was a dialogue distorted by his anticlericalism and willingness to judge his characters from the perspective of the *philosophes*.

Leopold von Ranke's distaste for Enlightenment theorising (which he blamed for the French Revolution) led him to reject any historical writing which imposed the values of its own time on the past. His influence short-circuited Enlightenment-style interest in structures and a tendency to raid the past for examples of the laws of human behaviour in society. In Ranke's terms, historical explanation was to rest upon the sources. Given the nature of the sources and the conservative and nationalistic viewpoint of many of Ranke's followers, the result was often narrative histories of the doings of the political élites. In Britain, however, the Rankean legacy can be seen in attacks on both Whig and Marxist interpretations of the past. The sweeping political narrative of the Whigs was objectionable because it imposed a pattern of progress towards liberal parliamentary democracy on the past and so failed to allow the past to speak on its own terms. The determinist philosophy of Marxism was rejected as a fundamentally unhistorical imposing of present-day theories on a past which must be allowed to explain itself. This suspicion of the teleological (see page 66) narrative (Whigs) and teleological analysis of structures (Marxists) led to a type of historical writing which was characteristically narrow in scope and generally focused on the motivations and behaviours of the élites. Namier's detailed scholarship is rather misleadingly known as 'structural analysis', but relies instead on detailed analysis, not of structures, but of the personalities and ambitions of individuals.

As for Marxist historiography itself, it is indeed heavily analytical. But, in seeking answers to problems, its reliance on historical determinism has the effect of dictating both the problems and the answers to them. A good example of the dangers is the controversy surrounding the young American historian David Abraham. He wrote a book on Weimar Germany which sought to explore the problem of the relationship between big business and the rise of Hitler. The traditional Marxist answer would be to argue that big business and Hitler served each others' needs. Sure enough, Abraham came up with evidence to support this thesis. However, his good faith was called into question by non-Marxist scholars who checked his references and alleged that he had deliberately distorted the evidence.[2] Whatever the truth of the matter, it is likely enough that Abraham was the victim of the trap gaping for those who impose a model on the past without giving priority to the way in which the past differs from the model. This is not to dismiss the value of Marxist historiography. It provided and continues to provide a corrective to the failure of narrative history to explore the relationship between a society's institutions, value-systems, culture and its economic base.

An attack on narrative history from a different perspective is a feature of the so-called *Annales* school of historians. As we saw in Chapter 4, *Annales* historians advocated an inter-disciplinary approach which analysed the shaping of society by long-term trends (*structure*) and rejected event-centred history as relatively unimportant. Traditional narratives had little part to play in the search for 'total history'. *Annales* history, with a very few exceptions such as Le Roy Ladurie's *Montaillou*, is never going to appeal to a popular readership. But it has, nevertheless, exposed the limitations of traditional story-type history by showing us that history need not be political narrative. Even so, *Annales* historians have arguably gone too far in rejecting events: a failure to integrate structural history with a discussion of events generally means that the role of the individual simply disappears.

It is tempting to assume that the various problems of narrative and analytical history can be solved by combining the two. This practice is common enough in academic history. Sometimes, the historian offers a narrative of events followed by an 'analytical' chapter. It is, perhaps, open to doubt how well this works. Narrative is unlikely to be devoid of analysis, and analytical passages are rarely without narrative. Blending the two may be the better way, and a recognition that historical explanation needs both events and structures, but with a discussion of how the two interconnect. This can be done. I remember getting a reading-list when starting my undergraduate course, and picking off the shelves Sir Richard Southern's *The Making of the Middle Ages*. I was hooked immediately. Southern managed to offer a riveting narrative whilst allowing the reader new to medieval history to understand the structures - and the fascination - of medieval society.

There is of course, a fundamental problem which may render the discussion of narrative and analytical history meaningless. This conclusion has rested on the assumption that history can make a genuine contribution to understanding truth - in this case, about the past. As we saw in Chapter 5, postmodernists would dismiss any such contention. To the postmodernist, the distinction between narrative and analysis, between event-centred history and structural history, is more of a distinction in style than in closeness to the truth. However, our discussion of postmodernism concluded that it rested upon questionable linguistic theories, that it tried to exploit methods of reason and logic that it denied to its opponents, and that its relativism was morally and philosophically unacceptable. But I also suggested that historians stood to gain from recognising the extent to which both their sources and their own writings are distorted by the kinds of style (and content) we generally associate with fiction (see pages 128-131).

3 The Value of History

If we ask a question about the value of history, we should also ask 'value for whom?' After all, are we talking about the value of history as a form of academic study? If so, do we discuss its value for school students, for university students, or for salaried historians? Can we assume that its value for each group is the same? Or are we talking about the value of history for those engaged in politics, where there might be lessons to learn from the past? Or about the proverbial man or woman in the street whose acquaintance with history as an academic subject may be extremely limited or even non-existent, but for whom history in the sense of 'the past' may mean a great deal? The short answer is that we should talk about them all. Sadly, few of the historians discussed in earlier chapters gave much attention to the needs of everyone.

4 History and Personal, Group and National Identity

It is, perhaps, crushingly obvious that we are the product of our own past: our experiences, real or imagined, help to shape the people we are. On my desk as I type are tangible reminders of my own past - in particular, some bits and pieces from an album I was looking at a few days ago: a student railcard with the photograph of a younger me, a photograph of myself and three friends standing soaked to the skin in Rome. Around the room are other photographs: my wedding day, my daughters and so on. We seem to have the desire to hang on to tangible aspects of our own past to give us a sense of rootedness, and therefore a sense of identity. The adopted child who, after many years, seeks out her natural parents may do so because she has a sense of a gap in her past which, in her own present, makes her feel incomplete. An older person, newly bereaved, can find that the trauma of loss generates memories which, in their vividness, help a little to fill in the emptiness. And in *The Drowned and the Saved*, Primo Levi commented on the importance to him of his memories of studying the poet Dante as he struggled to survive each day as a prisoner in the death camp of Auschwitz.

> They made it possible for me to re-establish a link with the past, saving it from oblivion and reinforcing my identity.

A sense of the past can confirm cultural as well as personal identity. According to David Lowenthal, the American tourist, from a comparatively new country, visits the Europe of his ancestors to 'feel at home in time'.[3] America, in fact, is an excellent example of how history can help to foster a sense of national identity in a country with a limited usable past. When the former colonists declared independence from Britain following the American Revolution of 1775-83, they explicitly rejected a past which was colonial and therefore British. However, within a generation of the Declaration of Independence, they had created a history for themselves - one in which the first settlers had deliberately set out to reject the values of the Old World in favour of a democratic vision of individual liberty.[4] This was bad history but very useful myth. It could be adapted for the countless immigrants of the nineteenth century, who were offered a clear image of what it meant to be an American: the freedom-loving pioneer of the American frontier whose hard work, self-reliance and love of family had shaped the nation.

A nation whose identity is under threat might also benefit from what Eric Hobsbawm has called 'invented traditions'. The Act of Union of 1707 between the crowns of England and Scotland was widely seen in Scotland as the first step towards the absorption of the Scottish way of life into that of her more powerful neighbour. Industrialisation seemed to be the agent of English cultural imperialism as railways brought the London newspapers - and so the London world-view - to some of the remoter reaches of Scotland. The wealth and glamour of London were enticing to many Scots, but the price was assimilation to English ways. One way to counter such a threat would be to encourage pride in Scottish culture and traditions, so that those exposed to English culture would not be seduced into seeing their own as inferior. Conveniently, the sensational discovery of a great epic written by a certain Ossian in the Gaelic tongue of Scotland's distant past appeared to meet that need. In fact, Ossian's poem was an 'invented tradition' - or, in other words, a fake. It was penned in the 1760s by James Macpherson to give his fellow-Scots a literary tradition to rival that of the English. Hugh Trevor-Roper has provocatively argued that two other trappings of the supposed Gaelic past, the kilt and the tartan, are similarly unhistorical inventions serving as a barrier to the loss of national identity.[5]

Myth in the service of national feeling can be extremely dangerous. The horrors of ethnic cleansing in the early 1990s in the former Yugoslavia were fed by the use of historical myth. In 1389, at the battle of Kosovo Field, a multinational Christian force was defeated by the largely Islamic armies of the Ottoman empire. In the second half of the nineteenth century, the new kingdom of Serbia made use of the Kosovo defeat to claim that the defeated leader, Tsar Lazar, was a Christian martyr who preferred a heavenly to an earthly crown. His glory was transmitted to the Serbian church and people, and that multinational army somehow became a Serbian one. And, by a further leap of fantasy, the concept of the holy nation of Serbia was used to justify expansionist ambitions at the expense of Albania. In 1986, Tsar Lazar's bones were exhumed and carried in grisly procession through Serbian villages with the intention of encouraging Serbs to fight their enemies. And their enemies were virtually everyone: the decadent West, the Roman Catholic Church, the Albanians, Croats, Muslims. In 1989 - the 600th anniversary of Kosovo - a mass rally was held on the site of the battle. President Milosevic and his Generals exploited nationalist frenzy to propel Serbs into war against their former partners in Yugoslavia. The horrors of Bosnia were the direct result.

5 Learning the Lessons of the Past: Can History Teach Political Lessons?

As we have seen, many historians wrote with the assumption that history could and should be studied with profit by those involved in the higher levels of politics. But is this assumption a fair one? After all, many politicians believe that one can learn from history, and make decisions accordingly. The 'lessons of Munich' are frequently cited as a guide to the way in which countries should respond to aggression. Hindsight would seem to suggest that the British Prime Minister Neville Chamberlain was dangerously mistaken when he attempted to appease Hitler at the Munich conference in 1938: the failure to defend Czechoslovakia against Nazi Germany simply served to encourage Hitler's expansionism and therefore led to the Second World War. Had Britain stood up to Hitler at that point (or preferably earlier, say over the remilitarisation of the Rhineland in 1936), then there would have been no invasion of Poland and therefore no war.

This all seems abundantly clear: identify a dictator who is getting friskily aggressive, and stamp on him at the first opportunity. But unfortunately there are a number of flaws in this kind of analogy which suggest that politicians are unwise to act as if Munich provides a fundamental rule of foreign policy. The first is that the condemnation of Chamberlain and his predecessors fails to take into account the actual historical context. Appeasement was probably the only viable course of action up to and including 1938. British public opinion was opposed to war. British interests were not directly involved in the fate of Czechoslovakia. Failing to put past events into their historical context makes analogies meaningless, and there have indeed been victims of what might be called the 'Munich Syndrome'. In 1956, the British PM Sir Anthony Eden came to the conclusion that Gamel Abdel Nasser, the ruler of Egypt, was a Middle Eastern version of Hitler. Eden interpreted Nasser's decision to nationalise the British-owned Suez Canal as a first step towards securing a stranglehold on the oil-supplies of the West. With the perils of appeasement fresh in his mind - he had been foreign secretary to Chamberlain - he decided to launch an airborne attack on the Suez Canal Zone in November 1956. In so doing, he alienated the United States, which simply rejected Eden's analogy. And with reason. In comparing Nasser to Hitler and Suez to Czechoslovakia in 1938, Eden had failed to take account of the entirely different historical circumstances. His analogy ignored the genuine grievances of Nasser over the legacy of colonialism. Under pressure from the USA, and in the background of threats from the Soviet Union, Britain (and her ally France) were forced to withdraw. The abject humiliation of his country, the breakdown in his already impaired health, and the sad evasions in his autobiography *Full Circle*, are all abundant testimony to the disasters which befell Eden when he attempted to learn simplistic lessons from history.

This is not to say that some good does not come out of politicians applying their wayward analogies in the attempt to learn from the past. The Munich/Hitler analogy was inevitably applied to the Iraqi dictator Saddam Hussein and his invasion of Kuwait in 1990. The freeing of Kuwait under the American-led forces of the United Nations would be seen by many as a good. But the problem is that politicians applying lessons from history are really just engaging in a game of Russian roulette. Sometimes they can be lucky, sometimes not. Success has little to do with the accuracy or otherwise of their analogies, which are generally never thought through anyway.

This is not to say that an understanding of history cannot help guide political behaviour. It is difficult to see how any effective diplomacy could take place without a firm understanding of the historical background of the countries involved. And, on an everyday level, political behaviour in a democracy must be informed by an historical perspective. When a political party in Britain, say, makes pledges to protect - or to reform - the National Health Service, then only a sense of history can give the voter an understanding of what the NHS is, what its aims were and how the parties treated it in the past.

6 The Role of the Professional Historian: in what ways, if any, might the historian contribute to society?

From what has been said in the previous section, it is clear that those who write history have great potential power, and with that power comes responsibility. The writing of nationalist or racist myth can lead to frightful evil. As Hobsbawm memorably puts it,

> ... bad history is not harmless history. It is dangerous. The sentences typed on apparently innocuous keyboards may be sentences of death.[6]

But we can put this more positively. It is the duty of the historian to expose myth: the more dangerous the myth, the more peremptory the duty. The obligation is there whether or not the historian's warning voice is likely to be heard. The strength of myth may well survive academic protest, but who is to know what the longer-term effects of such protest might be?

The historian, then, has very much a warning voice. This also applies to the Munich syndrome. The false analogy must be exposed, and it is the historian who has the expertise so to do. Now, this inevitably requires scholarly objectivity - one might say in the Rankean manner - but, unlike many followers of Ranke, the historian should consider the needs of his own times and own society. As we have seen, the present asks questions of the past, and the historian cannot leave it to others with vested interests who want to dictate the answers as well as the questions. I want to make use of Roy Porter's insight on this point, because he provides a most revealing example of historians seeking to answer questions of grave urgency. When the British government was confronting the AIDS crisis in the 1980s, it was faced with a dilemma. Should AIDS tests be made compulsory in the supposedly more vulnerable sections of society? What restrictions might be placed on the sexual conduct of sufferers? The Department of Health and Social Security requested advice from historians, and it is at least possible that harsh measures were not imposed because historians pointed to the public outcry that had greeted attempts by the Victorian authorities to impose medical inspections and custodial sentences on prostitutes carrying sexually transmitted diseases. Porter comments:

> For the health of history, it is crucial that historians.... recognise their responsibilities to meeting public needs.... Otherwise we will be treated

with deserved contempt, as being guilty of a prissy dereliction of duty.
The AIDS crisis is only one of the many issues where the public and
5 politicians look to history for illumination, ideas, and help. It is up to us
not to let them down.[7]

Indeed. But are there no other justifications for the professional
historian? After all, those whose specialisms lie in the remoter past
may find their knowledge is little in demand as a way of meeting
contemporary needs. Knowledge, perhaps: but the skills which historians teach are essential to a healthy society. The study of history is
food for the mind. It clearly demands and encourages a whole range
of skills, including those of analysis, synthesis and communication
(despite, one has to say, the wilful obscurity of some of its practitioners). Of course, one might argue that other disciplines can do
exactly the same. Perhaps. But unlike, say, the sciences, the best
history calls upon a mixture of imagination and empathy which is
stimulated by an awareness that one is dealing with human beings in
their wonderful complexity. History cannot set up experiments to test
its hypotheses, and has to make do with evidence which is incomplete.
This is a strength, since it encourages rigour in the exploiting of what
is available but discourages the arrogance of thinking that one has
found the 'truth'. It certainly encourages the critical spirit which is a
marked feature of a healthy democracy. Students of history are less
likely than most to fall for media propaganda.

7 And Finally ...

I recall a recent conversation with a colleague teaching an introductory historiography course. He commented that the students needed
some time to escape from the attitude of mind that the study of
history was something one did without thinking about what it was or
why one did it. They wanted, in fact, to be told the answers and the
facts ready, no doubt, for the next essay. This is a pity. Their engage-
ment with history would be little more than a synthesising of relevant
information: 'cut-and-paste history', indeed.

I am afraid that those who want the answers handed to them in pre-
digested form will have found this book difficult to slide past the
molars. In fact, there have been very few answers, but lots of questions. We have considered the nature and value of this subject, and
have looked at how historians past and present have tackled their task
of making intelligible that which has gone for ever. We have seen
those who would restrict history to the military and political deeds of
the élites: we have seen those who wanted to write the history of everything. We have studied those who see history as an essentially fictional
activity, and those who claim that, whilst it cannot recover the whole
truth, it gets mighty close. We have discussed how history which is
demonstrably false might do great good, and how history which is

demonstrably false might do great harm. We have seen that history is inescapable, but have warned of the dangers of escaping to it and so rejecting the present. We have looked at the many ways in which the past has been explained: by those who claim to make use of theories embodying laws of behaviour or of history itself, and by those who want to let the past speak without the distortion of theory.

Disagreement is surely the life-blood of the subject called history. It is an argument about the past, and an argument that can only die if either of the following occur:

1. An explanation of the past is imposed upon a society and accepted as beyond further dispute.
2. History is seen and widely accepted as an activity which merely serves immediate needs or prejudices of particular groups, and which cannot be judged as true or false in any way.

Neither have occurred, and I trust they never will.

References

1 C.V. Wedgwood, *The King's Peace 1637-1641* (BCA, 1974)
2 The Abraham case is discussed in Richard Evans, *In Defence of History* (Granta, 1997), pp.116-124.
3 David Lowenthal, *The Past is a Foreign Country* (Cambridge University Press, 1985), p.37.
4 See in particular the chapter 'History Makes a Nation' in Joyce Appleby *et al., Telling the Truth about History* (Norton, 1995), pp.91-125.
5 Hugh Trevor-Roper, in Hobsbawm and Ranger (eds.), *The Invention of Tradition* (Cambridge University Press, 1992), pp.15-41.
6 Eric Hobsbawm, *On History* (Weidenfeld & Nicolson, 1997), p.277.
7 Roy Porter, in Juliet Gardiner (ed.), *The History Debate* (Collins & Brown, 1990), pp.20-1.

Making notes on 'Conclusion: Types of Explanation and the Value of History"

The first part of the conclusion tackles the issue of the different types of historical writing, and offers a distinction between narrative and analytical history. Notes can therefore take the form of a definition of the two types, with examples. Notes on sections on the value of history can be compiled in the now familiar diagram form.

Writing essays on 'Conclusion: Types of Explanation and the Value of History'

The first part of this concluding chapter will be useful to supplement your answers on the more wide-ranging style of question, such as:

1. 'How far should historians concentrate on writing the history of events? In your answer, refer to at least two historians from differing traditions or schools of history.'

The second part of the conclusion enables you to tackle questions on history and national identity, history and myth and the value of the study of history. Questions can be extremely varied.

2. 'History can act as a stabilising influence on society: it can also destroy it completely.' Comment on this view.

3. 'The study of history is not a luxury, but a necessity.' To what extent do you agree with this view?

4. 'History should be studied so that we grow to understand the world in which we live.' Is this an adequate justification for the study of history?

5. 'Humankind needs history, and it does not matter how true that history is.' Comment on this view of the value of history.

6. 'Historical research is valuable only in so far as it provides intellectual satisfaction for the researcher.' How far do you agree with this view?

7. 'The most important - and only real - justification for studying history is that it is fun.' Comment on this view.

Hopefully, you will have noticed that some questions require you to consider a narrow aspect of history, be it 'research' or 'the study of history'. One of the familiar problems with 'value of history' questions is that students tend to churn out a prepared answer covering all possible values without anchoring their responses in the question itself. This is virtually re-writing the question to suit oneself, and examiners do not like it one bit. I suggest you write plans and introductions for any three of these questions which seem to you to demand differing approaches.

It is also possible that you might be asked a question about the purpose of school or college history. This will require you to make specific use of your knowledge of different historical periods and themes, but you should also exploit the ideas presented in this chapter. For example, one might argue that school history should prepare a student to participate in the political life of this country. Consider what periods of history would be most useful to study, but also consider the intellectual skills which a thinking member of society needs. What approaches to history and which topics would encourage the development of such skills? Take propaganda or media distortion - what might one study to see these exposed? Given that history does seem necessary to root oneself in time, should one study national history in a fundamentally chronological way? And, in a liberal and multi-cultural society, should one study other cultures? Should one study the way in which myths develop? Perhaps an examination of the development of racist ideology culminating in the Holocaust might prove useful. Write a plan for question 8.

8. 'It is vital for students to study history up to the age of 16, as long as it encourages a sense of national identity.' Comment on this view.

Further Reading

There are a number of relatively accessible books which cover some of the same themes as *History and the Historians*. Arthur Marwick's *The Nature of History* (Macmillan, third edition, 1989) is a book of some 400 pages which makes a gallant attempt to cover historiography, controversy in history, the historians at work and the relationship between history and other disciplines. It is very useful to dip into. John Tosh's *The Pursuit of History* (Longman, second edition, 1991) is narrower in scope, but particularly good on the value of history and on history and theory (especially on Marxism). Richard J. Evans' *In Defence of History* (Granta, 1997) offers a splendid gallop through historiography in the first chapter, although most of this work is a vigorous attack on postmodernism. For those readers who insist on reading more on postmodernism and who enjoy a tussle with a remarkably idiosyncratic and opaque style, look no further than Keith Jenkins. *Re-thinking History* (Routledge, 1991) is to be preferred to his *On 'What is History?'* (Routledge, 1995) - largely because it is shorter. *History and the Historians* is itself a version of my longer and somewhat more complex *The Past and its Presenters* (Hodder & Stoughton, 1998). The latter includes a full bibliography and a chapter made up of transcripts of interviews with two practising historians who reflect on several of the themes of the book.

Strongly recommended are the various studies in the *Historians on Historians* series (Weidenfeld & Nicolson): Roy Porter's *Edward Gibbon: Making History* (1988); John Gould's *Herodotus* (1989) and Linda Colley's *Namier* (1989).

Another excellent series is the Oxford *Past Masters*. The authors compress much learning into a hundred or so pages. I particularly like Quentin Skinner's *Machiavelli* (1981), J.W. Burrow's *Gibbon* (1985) and Peter Singers's *Marx* (1980).

The development of the *Annales* school can be traced in Peter Burke's *The French Historical Revolution: The Annales School, 1929-89* (Polity, 1990).

Excellent discussions of the use and abuse of history can be found in Hobsbawm and Ranger (eds.), *The Invention of Tradition* (Cambridge University Press, 1984); Linda Colley, *Britons: Forging the Nation 1707-1837* (Yale University Press, 1992) and, for America, in chapters 3 and 4 of Appleby, Hunt and Jacob, *Telling the Truth about History* (Norton, 1994). For a discussion of the uses of history in its broadest sociological and psychological sense, see David Lowenthal, *The Past is a Foreign Country* (Cambridge University Press, 1985).

There are a number of convenient collections of extracts from the writings of the great historians: Michael Grant, *Readings in the Classical Historians* (Scribner's Sons, 1992), Peter Burke, *The Renaissance Sense of the Past* (Edward Arnold, 1969) and Fritz Stern, *The Varieties of History: From Voltaire to the Present* (Macmillan, second edition, 1970). The Penguin Classics series is invaluable for the works of individual historians such as Herodotus, Thucydides, Polybius, Livy, Bede, some of Machiavelli's works, Gibbon and Macaulay.

Index